Sports Law in Slovenia

Sports Law in Slovenia

Jernej Podlipnik

This book was originally published as a monograph in the International Encyclopaedia of Laws/Sports Law.

Founding Editor: Roger Blanpain
General Editor: Frank Hendrickx
Volume Editor: Michele Colucci

Wolters Kluwer

Published by:
Kluwer Law International B.V.
PO Box 316
2400 AH Alphen aan den Rijn
The Netherlands
E-mail: international-sales@wolterskluwer.com
Website: lrus.wolterskluwer.com

Sold and distributed by:
Wolters Kluwer Legal & Regulatory U.S.
7201 McKinney Circle
Frederick, MD 21704
United States of America
Email: customer.service@wolterskluwer.com

ISBN 978-94-035-3150-2

e-Book: ISBN 978-94-035-3151-9
web-PDF: ISBN 978-94-035-3152-6

The Author

Jernej Podlipnik graduated in Law from University of Ljubljana, acquired his master's degree from University of Maribor and Doctor's degree from University of Ljubljana. For his master's and doctoral theses, the author focused on law and sports. For his master's thesis, he dealt with the legal and tax status of athletes and for the latter, he focused on issues relating to sport clubs.

Currently he is working as an independent tax consultant and as an Assistant Professor at the Graduate School of Government and European Studies in Kranj (Slovenia) where he lectures on Administrative Process Law, Administrative Dispute Law, Tax Process Law and Tax Law. The author also lectures on Tax Law at Faculty of Law (University of Ljubljana).

The Author

Table of Contents

List of Abbreviations

CAS	Court of Arbitration for Sport
COE	Council of Europe
EC	European Commission
EU	European Union
FIFA	International Federation of Association Football
FIS	International Ski Federation
IBU	International Biathlon Union
IFAB	International Football Association Board
IOC	International Olympic Committee
NATO	North Atlantic Treaty Organization
NPC	Sports Federation for the Disabled of Slovenia – Paralympic Committee of Slovenia
OCS	Olympic Committee of Slovenia – A Federation of Sport Associations
OECD	Organisation for Economic Co-operation and Development
SFRY	Socialist Federative Republic of Yugoslavia
SLOADO	Slovenian Anti-Doping Organisation
UEFA	Union of European Football Associations
UN	United Nations
UNESCO	United Nations Educational, Scientific and Cultural Organization
VAT	Value Added Tax
WADA	World Anti-Doping Agency
WADC	World Anti-Doping Code

List of Abbreviations

Acknowledgements

I am honoured and delighted to be able to contribute to this prestigious encyclopaedia. The task was quite challenging since, in Slovenia, this field of law has been unduly quite neglected, and therefore the literature on this topic is scarce. It seems that more and more lawyers in Slovenia are becoming aware of the importance of sports law, but it will take some more time before sports law reaches the place it deserves. I hope that this monograph will contribute to this goal. Since its initial release, many legal sources have been changed. Most important for this text is that in 2017 the legislator passed a new Sports Act. Its content is not revolutionary, but its predecessor did not regulate certain issues (e.g., employment).

This monograph is written within limits set by the publisher. We are focusing on four main parts that the publisher required – organization, status, doping and commerce; although many other fields of law (tort law, criminal law, dispute resolution, etc.) that also are connected to sports could be interesting for the readers. To ensure uniform content in all sports law monographs, we have deliberately omitted these legal issues.

I would like to thank the editor and publisher for their patience, since I was not able to finish my work on time. Lastly, I would like to thank my family for supporting me and understanding that writing such text takes a lot of precious time. I promise I will do more sports and less law.

Vrhnika, Slovenia, 10 August 2020

Acknowledgements

General Introduction

§1. General Background

1. Slovenia is a small country located in Southern Central Europe. It borders Italy to the west, Austria to the north, Croatia to the south and southeast and Hungary to the northeast. It also borders the Adriatic Sea to the southwest. Slovenia has a population of approximately 2 million inhabitants, and it covers 20,273 square kilometres (7,827 square miles). Slovenia is a member of the European Union (EU), Organisation for Economic Co-operation and Development (OECD), Council of Europe (COE) and North Atlantic Treaty Organization (NATO). Its capital and largest city is Ljubljana.

2. Slovenia has been independent since 1991. Before that Slovenia was one of the republics of former Socialist Federative Republic of Yugoslavia (SFRY). Since independence, Slovenia has been a parliamentary democratic republic, which is governed by the rule of law and has also been a social state (Articles 1, 2 and 3 of the Slovenian Constitution).[1] The Constitution (Article 4) states that Slovenia is a territorially unified and indivisible state, but on the other hand guarantees local self-government (Article 9). There are 212 municipalities established in Slovenia, and most of them are quite small and often unable to provide quality public services for their citizens.

3. The legal system in Slovenia is a part of the continental legal systems with the strong influence of German law and legal order with the impact of the socialist legal system. There are historic reasons for this as the territory of today's Slovenia was a part of Austrian Empire for a long time, and from the end of the Second World War, it was a part of SFRY as already mentioned.[2]

1. English translation of the Slovenian Constitution is available at https://www.us-rs.si/media/constitution.pdf (accessed 30 Jul. 2019). We note that since this translation an article that guarantees the right to drinking water (Art. 70.a) was added to the text, but this is not directly relevant for this monograph.
2. More on this topic, *see* M. Čarni and Š. Košak, *A Guide to the Republic of Slovenia Legal System and Legal Research*, 2006, https://www.nyulawglobal.org/globalex/Slovenia.html (accessed 30 Jul. 2019) and http://www.servat.unibe.ch/icl/si__indx.html (accessed 30. Jul. 2019).

4. According to the research made by the European Commission (EC) in 2013,[3] citizens of Slovenia are quite active physically in comparison with citizens of other Member States. Taking into account the small population, one can say that Slovenian professional athletes are very successful. For example, in the last winter Olympic Games in PyeongChang (2018), they received two[4] medals and in the last summer Olympic Games in Rio de Janeiro (2016) they received four.[5] Names like Luka Dončić and Goran Dragić (basketball), Peter Prevc (ski jumping), Anže Kopitar (ice hockey), Primož Roglič and Tadej Pogačar (cycling), Janja Garnbret (climbing) Samir Handanović, Jan Oblak and Josip Iličić (football), Ilka Štuhec (alpine skiing), Tina Trstenjak (judo) are known not only among fans of those sports but also among people who only occasionally watch sports.

5. The national teams in basketball and handball are among the best in the world and commonly participate in European and World championships. Slovenian national basketball team is a current European champion (Istanbul, 2017). In football, Slovenia is not so successful, but still played on one European championship (2000) and two World championships (2002 and 2010). The reason for a smaller success in football is probably due to poorly developed national league with only few stable clubs (e.g., Maribor[6] and Olimpija).

6. Slovenia hosts and has hosted some important international sports events. These annual events are mostly connected to winter sports (ski jumping in Planica and alpine skiing in Kranjska Gora and Maribor). The above-mentioned events are very successful and popular among participants and spectators, not only Slovenian but also spectators from all over Europe who attend these events. The biggest sports events that Slovenia has hosted were the European Handball Championship in 2004 and the European Basketball Championship in 2013. They made a great impact on the popularity of these sports and were also successfully organized.

7. As sport spectators, Slovenians are a tough crowd. They strongly cheer for their athlete, club or national team when successful, but soon lose interest when results are not as brilliant.

8. Lately Slovenians have started occupying important positions in international sports organizations. Mr Aleksander Čeferin is the President of Union of European Football Associations (UEFA) and Dr Janez Kocijančič was, before he died in 2020, the European Olympic Committees President, if I mention just two of them who are probably the most influential.

---

3. European Commission, Sport and Physical Activity. Special Eurobarometer, 2018, https://ec.europa.eu/commfrontoffice/publicopinion/index.cfm/ResultDoc/download/DocumentKy/82432 (accessed 30 Jul. 2019).
4. The number is lower than in Sochi (2014) where Slovenian athletes received eight medals. The reason for the lower number of medals is the retirement of some of Slovenia's best athletes.
5. The same number as in London (2012).
6. In season 2014–2015, Football club Maribor repeated its success from season 1999–2000 and qualified for UEFA Champions League. This is a great success for Maribor and also for Slovenian football taking into account financial inputs into this club.

9. Lack of funds is also an important factor. Since Slovenia is such a small country, sponsors are not as keen to invest on Slovenian athletes, clubs or national teams as they are with the greater nations. This is the reason the state also employs athletes in the ministries; thus enabling them to professionally practice sports where athletes do not earn enough money to finance their careers themselves.

§2. Sources of Sports Law

10. This monograph is titled Sports Law, but among Slovenian scholars the term 'Sport and the Law' is preferred and is supposed to be more specific, because we cannot (at least not yet) speak about a special independent legal discipline,[7] but can address:

– the public rules of traditional legal disciplines (constitutional law, civil law, criminal law, commercial law, etc.) that are also applicable in relation to sports;
– the special public rules that govern just sport relations; and
– the special (autonomous) rules of sport organizations.[8]

Despite this terminological issue, which is mostly theoretical, we will later on in this monograph use the term 'Sports Law'. By it we are referring to the general and abstract legal principles and rules that apply to sport relations.

11. Literature on sport legal issues in Slovenia is scarce. Only one out of three Slovenian law faculties has a course on this matter. Besides the first issue of this monograph, only one monograph that deals with sports and the law was published, but is only available in Slovene, and the same applies for most of the other published articles. In fact, most of the available literature comes from graduation, master's or doctoral theses that deal with more or less narrow sport legal issues. Some of them are quoted and listed in this monograph. This edition is actually the second publication in English that deals with some of the sport legal issues in Slovenia.

12. The word 'sport' is not mentioned in the Constitution of the Republic of Slovenia.[9] This does not mean that Constitutional provisions are not applicable to the field of sports. As we will see later on in this monograph, the right of assembly and association (Article 42) directly influences organization of sport.[10] Other constitutional provisions such as free enterprise (Article 72), taxes (Article 147) have a more indirect influence. Human rights and fundamental freedoms play an important role in the Slovenian legal system (Article 5); they must also be taken into consideration when dealing with legal sport issues. This applies not only to the human rights and fundamental freedoms mentioned in the Slovenian Constitution but also the ones that Slovenia has committed to protect with international treaties (Articles

7. V. Bergant Rakočević, *Športno pravo – nova disciplina?*, Pravna praksa, No. 36/2001, 16–17.
8. M. Ilešič, *Družbeni in pravni vidiki športa*, 39 (V. Bergant Rakočević ed., *Šport & pravo*, GV Založba 2008).
9. Official Journal of the Republic of Slovenia, Nos 33/91-I, 42/97, 66/00, 24/03, 69/04, 69/04, 69/04, 68/06, 47/13, 47/13 and 75/16.
10. J. Tratnik, *Pregled pozitivne pravne zakonodaje, ki ureja šport*, 5 (M. Ilešič & T. Jagodic eds, Olimpijski komite Slovenije 1994).

8 and 15). We will not make an in-depth analysis of every constitutional provision that could potentially have an impact on sports. The ones that are important for the chapters covered in this monograph will be dealt with later on in each of the parts.

13. Slovenia has also entered into a few international treaties that are important in the field of sport. These are, for example, two COE treaties: European Convention on Spectator Violence and Misbehaviour at Sports Events and, in particular, at Football Matches of 1985[11] and Anti-Doping Convention of 1989.[12] Although they were signed and ratified in SFRY, they are binding to Slovenia. Their influence on current Slovenian legislation will be dealt with later on in the relevant chapters of this monograph. Besides that, Slovenia has also concluded a United Nations (UN) International Convention against Doping in Sport.

14. In Slovenia, a special Sports Act[13] is implemented. It sets out the public interest in the field of sport, mechanisms for serving this public interest, responsible authorities and the conditions for carrying out professional work in sport, the rights of athletes, public sports facilities and outdoor natural sports grounds, sporting events, and databases and supervision in the field of sport (Article 1). Besides the Sports Act, two other special acts that deal with sports are worth mentioning: Bridging Insurance of Professional and Top Athletes Act[14] and Act Regulating the Supplement to Pensions for Work and Outstanding Achievements in Sports.[15] Certain general acts contain special provisions with rights and obligations connected to sports (e.g., Personal Income Tax Act).[16]

15. The public interest is specified in the national programme of sport. This is a strategic document of sports policy development planning which adopted for a period of ten years, that lays down:

- the public interest in the field of sport;
- objectives and priorities of the sports policy;
- sports programmes;
- investments in sports facilities and outdoor natural sports grounds;
- development, expert and research activities in sport;
- the organizational structure in sport;
- sporting events and the promotion of sport;
- social and environmental responsibilities in sport; and
- support mechanisms for sport.

---

11. Official Journal of SFRY, No. 9/90.
12. Official Journal of SFRY, No. 4/91.
13. Official Journal of the Republic of Slovenia, Nos 29/17 and 21/18. Unofficial Consolidated Text is available in English and Slovenian language at: http://www.pisrs.si/Pis.web/npbDocPdf?idPredpisa=ZAKO7129&idPredpisaChng=ZAKO6853&type=doc&lang=EN (accessed 30 Jul. 2019).
14. Official Journal of Slovenia, No. 82/15.
15. Official Journal of Slovenia, No. 34/17.
16. Official Journal of Slovenia, Nos 13/11 (Official Consolidated Text), 9/12, 24/12, 30/12, 40/12, 75/12, 94/12, 52/13, 96/13, 29/14, 50/14, 23/15, 55/15, 63/16, 69/17, 21/19 and 28/19.

The national programme must define measures and indicators to measure its implementation, lay down strategic, financial, staff and organizational guidelines that are essential for its implementation.

16. Although the national programme of sport is not a source of law, but a strategic document, it is worth mentioning, because it is a basis for annual sports programme plans (Articles 12–14 of the Sports Act) which are e essential for public funding.

17. From the public regulation perspective, other sports law issues are left for everyone to decide on their own, according to their interest. There are a number of other valid general public law acts that are important for sports in Slovenia.[17] The content of ones that are important for this monograph is presented later on in the relevant chapter.

18. Private regulation plays an important role in the field of sports law. Every sport organization has special (autonomous) rules of sport organizations that are general and abstract and that regulate the behaviour of legal subject (individuals and legal persons). It is not possible to deal with each one of them, hence the presentation in this monograph is limited to detailed presentation of two organizations (*see* §4 Limitations of this monograph below).

§3. Specificity of Sport

19. A theory that sport is a game and hence excluded from the law (so-called legal immunity of sport) is outdated. The relationship between the law (a system of legal norms) and sports is a so-called *and theme* (German *Und- Theme*) – a theme between the law and a certain life phenomena (in this case sport).[18] The term 'sports law' is therefore the entirety of legal norms that are significant to sports. These norms can either be set by the State (public law) or by private entities (e.g., sport associations) and individuals (private law).[19]

20. The classical and still, ever-current central (legal) question in the debate of sport in whether sport is 'special', and hence whether it deserves specific (special) treatment under law and to what extent and why.[20] Simplified – are general legal rules also applicable to sports?

---

17. Some on the homepage of Ministry of Education, Science and Sport, but are only available in Slovene: http://www.mizs.gov.si/si/zakonodaja_in_dokumenti/veljavni_predpisi_s_podrocja_sporta/ (accessed 30 Jul. 2019).
18. M. Ilešič, *Družbeni in pravni vidiki športa*, 36–37 (V. Bergant Rakočević ed., *Šport & pravo*, GV Založba 2008).
19. Cf. M. Kirschenhofer, *Sport als Beruf*, 5 (Peter Lang 2002).
20. Cf. R. Siekmann, *The Specificity of Sport: Sporting Exceptions in the EU Law*, 698 (Zbornik radova Pravnog fakulteta u Splitu 4/2012).

21. The answer is affirmative. The basic human rights guaranteed by constitutions and international treaties must be respected in sports. This is also true for the general legal principles such as *pacta sunt servanda, neminem ladere* and so on. It would be inappropriate to state that liability for damages, criminal liability, contract law, personality rights law, labour and social law, basic procedural guarantees (e.g., the right to a fair trial), etc. do not apply.[21] However, according to the proportionality test when applying the rules in factual situations particular features and characteristics of sport (e.g., rules of the game or *lex ludica*) should be respected.[22] Sometimes countries' special sports public rules deviate from the general rules (e.g., Slovenian Sports Act has special provisions regarding the employment relationships between athletes and clubs).[23]

22. The nature of sports as a social activity and its specific organization has led to creation of rules that are specific to sports. These special (autonomous) rules can be divided into two categories. The first are already mentioned rules of the game (*lex ludica*) that govern the course of sport competitions (technical or professional rules that are usually applied by referees). They are in the exclusive discretion of sport associations. The second are those autonomous rules that can collide with the above-mentioned basic human rights and general legal principles (e.g., interference of autonomous sports rules in the rights arising from the employment of an athlete). It is not always easy to set the line between these two groups, and this is made on a case-by-case basis.[24] It can be said that organization of sport on a national level, the principle of a single federation per sport, the pyramid structure of open competitions, separate competitions for men and women, voluntariness, the position of amateur sport, the interdependence between competing adversaries, the principle of equal opportunities and uncertainty of results (competitive balance), financial solidarity (especially, professional football), national teams of '(EU-)nationals', compensation schemes for young players (football), limitation of the number of participants in a competition (other than national teams), transfer deadlines in team sports, anti-doping rules, 'at home and away from home' rule (football), no multiple ownership in sport clubs and ticketing arrangements for safety reasons, are particular characteristics of sport(s) itself. At least from an EU law perspective.[25]

---

21. Cf. M. Ilešič, *Družbeni in pravni vidiki športa*, 39–41 (V. Bergant Rakočević ed., *Šport & pravo*, GV Založba 2008).
22. Cf. R. Siekmann, *The Specificity of Sport: Sporting Exceptions in the EU Law*, 723 (Zbornik radova Pravnog fakulteta u Splitu 4/2012).
23. To comply with the Slovenian Constitution such exceptions must be justified not to infringe the general equality before the law principle (Art. 14.2). Hence, the legislator does not have an absolute discretion when enacting special rules (that apply only to sports). His decision must not be arbitrary, therefore he has to show either that special (different) rule is necessary due to essential differences in legal relationship or that legal relations are not essentially different, but real and reasonable grounds exist that justify different legal treatment. Cf. F. Grad, I. Kaučič & S. Zagorc, *Ustavno pravo*, 746–747 (Pravna fakulteta 2016).
24. Cf. M. Ilešič, *Družbeni in pravni vidiki športa*, 31–42 (V. Bergant Rakočević ed., *Šport & pravo*, GV Založba 2008).
25. R. Siekmann, *The Specificity of Sport: Sporting Exceptions in the EU Law*, 723 (Zbornik radova Pravnog fakulteta u Splitu 4/2012).

§4. LIMITATIONS OF THIS MONOGRAPH

23. As noted above, this monograph only deals with some of the sport legal issues in Slovenia, namely those dealing with organization, status, doping and commerce in sport. The reader should therefore not take this monograph as all-encompassing.

24. These issues are dealt with at a basic level, explaining the valid rules and practise, without evaluating them from a theoretical perspective and suggesting on for the future regulation and practise. We believe this kind of evaluation would go beyond the purpose of this monograph.

25. Especially in first two parts (organization of sport and sport and employment) I write about sport organizations, so I must define this term. By sport organizations, I refer to those associations that directly or indirectly participate in professional or amateur sport competitions. Recreational sport is excluded. They are most commonly named sport clubs or just clubs, irrespective of their legal nature. National and international associations of sport clubs are also sport organizations in the sense of this monograph; sometimes simply referred to as sport federations. Sport associations or sport federations also participate in competitions as organizers and supervisors of national and international sport competitions. I will, however, in this monograph, not address other organizations that are a part of sport industry (sport marketing companies, manufacturers or traders of sporting equipment, organizers of sports betting, media that is covering only sports, etc.).

26. Since there are so many sport associations in Slovenia with special autonomous rules, it would have been impossible to present every one of them. I picked one individual and one collective sport.[26] I have chosen the rules of Ski Association of Slovenia and Football Association of Slovenia; the first one because it is the biggest sport association in Slovenia, and the second one because football is the most popular sport in the world. We note that autonomous rules of other sport associations may differ and that they cannot be generalized. However, in general, it can be said that rules of other sport organizations are in essence the same as those presented in this monograph.

27. Besides autonomous rules of these two associations we will, of course, also present the autonomous rules of Olympic Committee of Slovenia – A Federation of Sports Associations (OCS).

---

26. A differentiation between collective and individual sports is based on the number of participative competitors (S. Kostandinović & I. Kostandinović, *Pravo i sport*, 85 (Fakultet za menadžment u sportu 2007) and Z. Milić, *Sport i pravna regulativa u sportu*, 50 (Fakultet sporta i fizičkog vaspitivanja 2007)).

Part I. Organization of Sport

Chapter 1. Sports Governance

§1. Governmental Institutions and Bodies

28. Sports Act lays down the basis of sports governance in Slovenia. According to its provisions, several different governmental institutions and bodies have tasks and responsibilities in the provision of public interest in the field of sport. These tasks can be divided into two groups: first, financial conditions (public funding), and second, tax and administrative conditions. In this chapter institutions and bodies with financial tasks are presented as they are specified in detail in Sports Act. Unspecified (programme) provisions, according to which a favourable fiscal and administrative environment for sport should be provided, are not dealt with here but later on in the appropriate chapters.

29. Sports Act does not only determine the jurisdictions of governmental institutions and bodies but also of local communities that exercise the public interest in sport at the local level.[27]

I. National Level

30. On the top of the pyramid is the National Assembly (Parliament) that exercises the legislative function (Article 87 of the Constitution), and it determines the public interest through it.[28] The above-mentioned and briefly explained national programme[29] is also adopted by the National Assembly. This is logical since this institution consists of directly elected representatives of the people (voters). The Government prepares the proposal of the national programme on the basis of the draft written by the ministry responsible for sport (hereinafter: the Ministry).[30] To

27. According to the Constitution (Art. 140) local affairs which affect only the residents of each municipality are in original jurisdiction of local communities (local self-government). The state must refrain from interfering in municipalities' original jurisdictions.
28. National Assembly is therefore mainly responsible for providing a favourable fiscal and administrative environment for sport by adopting tax law acts and administrative law act that ensure these desirable objectives.
29. *See* General introduction, §2. Sources of Sports Law.
30. Slovenia does not have a separate ministry of sports. Within the Ministry of Education, Science and Sports, a Sports Directorate is organized. This Directorate performs tasks of the State, as defined by

ensure that decisions are not purely political Sports Act states that the Ministry must obtain the opinion of the Expert Council on Sport of the Republic of Slovenia (hereinafter: Council of Experts) and that OCS has to agree with the draft. If the OCS and the Ministry fail to reach the agreement, the Ministry can submit the draft to the Government for consideration provided it obtains the consent of the Council of Experts after the second reading.

31. The Government shall adopt action plan on implementation of the national programme. Before doing so, the Government must obtain a prior opinion by the Council of Experts and the agreement of the OCS. The action plan regulates in detail the actions and orientations of the national programme. If the agreement of the OCS is not obtained, the Government shall adopt the action plan subject to the consent of the Council of Experts after the second reading. To carry out the activities of the action plan that arise from the measures of the national programme, responsible bodies shall be designated together with time limits for their implementation. The action plan is adopted for the same period of time for which the national programme is adopted. The Government must submit a report to the National Assembly on the implementation of the national programme every two years. The Ministry writes a draft of such report.

32. The Minister responsible for sport (hereinafter: the Minister) determines the implementation of the action plan at the national level for individual calendar years through annual national sports programme. Annual sports programmes determine which content and which fields of sport are co-funded in individual calendar years and the amount of public funding provided from the national budget. Before determination, the Minister has to obtain the opinion of the Council of Experts and the OCS. If the Council of Experts and the OCS fail to deliver their opinions within a period of one month, the Minister may adopt the annual national sports programme without obtaining the mentioned prior opinions.

33. Public funds are then divided based on the annual programme. The contract is concluded with the beneficiaries. They are generally selected using a public tender; exceptionally they are selected without it.[31]

---

the Sports Act, such as tasks 'associated with the co-financing of sport programmes at the national level that are in the public interest, and the provision of the implementation of the Sports Act in the areas facilitating a smooth functioning of sports organisations and associations, the members of which are sports professionals, experts and athletes. Moreover, it monitors the implementation of the Sports Act, designs the necessary amendments and drafts implementing regulations and other acts ensuring smooth, systemic and financial support to sport'. (http://www.mizs.gov.si/en/areas_of_work/ (accessed 30 Jul. 2019))

31. Sports Act expressly determines in which cases public funds can be distributed without a public tender:

    (1) Preparations for and participation in the international multi-disciplinary sports competitions that are organized by the OCS or the NPC.
    (2) Participation in University Games or European university sports competitions and World and European University Championships organized by the Slovenian University Sports Association.

II. The Foundation for Funding Sports Organizations in the Republic of Slovenia

34. Not all public funds on a national level are distributed directly from the national (state) budget. In order to provide stable financing of sports which is independent of politics the National Assembly founded a separate public legal entity whose sole purpose is to finance Slovenian sports organizations.[32] This is the Foundation for Funding Sports Organizations in the Republic of Slovenia (hereinafter: Sports Foundation). Sports Foundation is a separate legal person with public powers – a so-called body exercising public powers (bearer of public authority).[33] It is a non-profit organization whose income must be used exclusively for its operation and its purpose of establishment (financing and co-financing of sports). To be able to perform the prescribed task, the National Assembly had to provide regular and direct funding of the Sports Foundation. Its main sources of income are concession fees and 5% of lottery ticket profits[34] according to the Gaming Act.[35]

35. Sports Foundation distributes its funds according to its own annual sports programme. In preparing and adopting the content of the annual programme (content and fields of sports), the Foundation has to take into consideration the structure and priorities set in the national programme and action plan. For the selection of beneficiaries, the same rules apply as for the distribution of funds on a national level.

III. Local Level

36. Slovenia municipal councils determine the implementation of the national programme at the local level for individual calendar years by adopting annual local sports programmes. Annual local sport programmes provide content in the fields of sport that are to be co-funded in individual calendar years and the amount of public funding to be provided from the local community budget, taking into consideration

---

(3) The implementation of the sports programme or field that is co-funded from the budget provided by an international sports organization or the EU and has been selected in a public tender conducted by an institution outside the Republic of Slovenia.

(4) Investments in public sports facilities and outdoor sports grounds if their significance exceeds the level of a local community, or if this is necessary for a harmonious development of the country and it is in the public interest, and the need for the construction or renovation of these sports facilities and outdoor natural sports grounds stems from the network of sports facilities and outdoor natural sports grounds.

32. Ownership Transformation of the Lottery of Slovenia Act (Official Journal of Slovenia, Nos 44/96, 47/97, 102/07, 26/11, 109/11, 58/12 and 29/17) and Decree establishing a Foundation for the Financing of Sports Organizations in the Republic of Slovenia (Official Journal of Slovenia, No. 9/98).
33. According to Art. 121 of the Constitution by law or on the basis thereof, legal entities and natural persons may be vested with the public authority to perform certain duties of the state administration.
34. In 2018 almost 96% of funds (Sports Foundation, Annual Report 2018, 41–45, http://www.fundacijazasport.org/si/files/default/Letno%20porocilo%20o%20delu%20Fundacije%20za%20sport%20v%20letu%202018.pdf (accessed 31 Jul. 2019).
35. Official Journal of Slovenia, Nos 14/11 (Official Consolidated Text), 108/12, 11/14 and 40/11.

the structure and priorities set in the national programme.[36] Before adopting the programme, municipal council had to obtain the opinion of the municipal sport federations if such exists in the respective municipality. Notwithstanding this demand, a municipal council may adopt the annual local sports programme without obtaining the mentioned prior opinion if a municipal sport federation fails to deliver it within a period of one month. Local municipalities distribute their funds through the procedure that is essentially the same as on a national level. Beneficiaries are as a rule selected through public tender, and exceptionally without it.

§2. National Olympic Committee and Sports Associations

I. Introduction

37. The same as elsewhere in Europe, Slovenian sport has a pyramid structure. Slovenia follows the so-called European Model of Sport. On top of the pyramid within Slovenia is the OCS, at least for the sport federations that are members of it. One step below are national sport federations (e.g., Ski Association of Slovenia, Football Association of Slovenia), which can be further divided into inter-municipal (regional) sport federations, but this is not always the rule. At the bottom of the pyramid structure are sport clubs.[37] Competing athletes can be members of sport clubs, but they do not have to be in order to compete for the clubs. Their legal relationship with the clubs can only be of a contractual nature, but often athletes must also be registered for certain club by national sport federation. The purpose of registration is mainly to prevent athletes to freely change registration whenever they please which could (especially in team sports) affect the fairness of competition.

38. Although this is not the main focus of this monograph, it must be noted that national Olympic committees and national sport federations are (usually) members of European or world sporting federations (International Olympic Committee (IOC), International Ski Federation (FIS), International Federation of Association Football (FIFA), etc.). In this way they are on a lower level of a larger (international) pyramid.[38]

II. Olympic Committee of Slovenia

39. According to Articles of Association[39] (Article 1), OCS is a central, non-governmental sport federation that combines national sport federations, local sport federation and other professional sport organizations in Slovenia. For each sport discipline, only one national sport federation can be a member of OCS. The same

36. Sports Act does not mention action plan, as municipalities are independent of the Government.
37. J. Podlipnik, *Pravni in davčni status športnih klubov* (PhD Thesis, Law faculty in Ljubljana 2010).
38. Cf. S. Gardiner et al., *Sports Law*, 151 (Cavendish Publishing Limited 2005).
39. Available only in Slovenian language at: https://www.olympic.si/datoteke/Pravila%20OKS-Z%C5%A0Z-Potrjena%20na%20Upravni%20enoti-SKENIRANA%20VERZIJA(1).PDF (accessed 1 Aug. 2019).

applies to local sport federations for the territory of each local community. Articles of Association also allow other natural (active and former athletes that actively participated in Olympic Games, Slovenian members of IOC) and legal (sponsors who are legal entities) to be its members, but the legality of this provision is questionable because it could be contrary to the Societies Act[40] (Article 16). From an international perspective, OCS is a member of IOC and is therefore obliged to follow all its rules and decisions.

40. By its legal status OCS is a union of sport federations according to the Societies Act. It is therefore a legal person of private law; hence, private law norms mostly apply to it. Interestingly Sports Act also defines OCS in Article 41: 'The OCS is an umbrella sports organization that is an integral part of the international Olympic movement and connects national and municipal sports federations and other sports organizations and is organized in accordance with the Societies Act.' Because of its importance for sports, Sports Act mentions OCS several times. Sports Act grants OCS certain public law rights, e.g., as a rule, consensus in adopting a national sports programme (Article 9) and its action plan (Article 10), the right to submit an opinion on the draft annual national sports programme (Article 12).

41. Membership in OCS is voluntary (Article 12.1 of Articles of Association), but in order to participate in competitions sport federations directly and other sports associations and clubs indirectly must become members. To become that, they must meet certain conditions stated in Article 13 of Articles of Association, among which is also a statement of acceptance and compliance with the rules and other acts of the OCS. Without signing this statement sport federations cannot become members of OCS (Article 16), and they can also be expelled from the organization if members do not comply with the rules and other acts of OCS (Articles 19 and 24).

42. Perhaps more than legal coercion, compliance with the rules of the OCS is also influenced by the fact that this organization directly or indirectly provides funding for some of its members' activities, which is why they are interested in complying with its rules.[41]

A. *OCS' Governing Bodies*

43. OCS' Articles of Association determine four governing bodies and their rights and responsibilities: General Assembly, Executive Committee, Supervisory Board and Disciplinary Commission.

40. Official Journal of the Republic of Slovenia, Nos 64/11 (Official Consolidated Text) and 21/18.
41. Cf. I. Crnić et al., *(Uvod u) športsko pravo*, 35 (Inženjerski biro 2009).

B. General Assembly

44. General Assembly is the OCS' highest authority. It is composed of:

- all representatives of national sport federations;
- thirty representatives of local sport federations;
- six representatives of sport federations and associations;
- one individual member;
- two active Olympic athletes, of which one is male and the other female; and
- two former Olympic athletes, of which one is male and the other female.

45. Most vital powers of the General Assembly are (e.g.):

- adopting and changing OCS' most important rules (e.g., Articles of Association);
- deciding on the annual accounts;
- electing and dismissing the president and vice-presidents of OCS, members of Executive Committee, Supervisory Board, Disciplinary Commission and Electoral Commission;[42] and
- deciding on the admission and exclusion of members of the OCS.

C. Executive Committee

46. Executive Committee manages the work of the OCS. It consists of twenty-five members. At least five of them must be female. The president and three vice-presidents of OCS that are separately elected by the General Assembly are automatically members of the Executive Committee. Articles of Association specify the composition of the Executive Board in order to ensure uniform representation of the members of the OCS, however, it gives more weight to Olympic sports. It also ensures that among Olympic sports individual and team sports and winter and summer sports are properly represented.

47. Most vital powers of the Executive Committee are (e.g.):

- preparing draft acts for adoption at the General Assembly;
- executing the resolutions of the General Assembly;
- determining the membership fee;
- appointing and dismissing the OCS's Secretary-General; and
- establishing the working bodies.

48. Articles of Association state that Executive Committee has several sub-bodies. This is logical as it is a large body itself and hence not always operational. Nonetheless, Executive Committee is entitled to establish a commission or a working group if needed for performing a task within its jurisdiction.

42. Electoral Commission is a special (internal) body of a General Assembly which is responsible for the proper conduct of the elections. It is therefore not an independent body of OCS.

49. The most important operational body is the Secretary-General. The Executive Committee appoints him or her on a proposal from the President. The Secretary-General is an executive function that is performed professionally.

D. Supervisory Board

50. Supervisory Board has three members and two deputies. The main tasks are:

– business review at least once a year;
– supervising the enforcement of decisions taken by OCS' bodies;
– controlling the legality of the work; and
– controlling financial operations.

E. Disciplinary Commission

51. Disciplinary Commission consists of three members and two deputies. Its task is to lead disciplinary proceedings and impose disciplinary sanctions according to disciplinary rules.

III. Sport Associations and Sport Federations

52. Sport federations and sport associations are legally specific forms of societies. According to Article 16 of the Societies Act, at least two societies may establish a federation or association (a union of societies). Members (i.e., general assembly) of all societies must make the decision. The same rule applies if a society would like to join a federation or association that is already established. Federations are legal entities; they have their own acts of association, their representative, etc. Members of a federation must have a legal form of association; other legal forms are prohibited. The same applies to individuals (natural persons), but as I have already mentioned, Articles of Association of OCS state otherwise and are in my opinion legally questionable.

53. Regardless of the fact if sport federations or associations are (directly or indirectly) members of OCS, they set the rules for the organization of sports on the territory they cover. In case of national sport federations, it is the territory of Slovenia and in other cases, these are narrower zones within the national territory. In any case, rules set by sport federations (associations) maintain the pyramid structure of sports. The federations are, in fact, associations of sport clubs that are participating in sport competitions and events organized by the federations. Sport clubs, their members and their registered athletes must comply with the rules set by sport federations. As members of these federations, sport clubs participate in a process of rules adoption, but since sport federations are (directly or indirectly) members of international sport federations they must also consider the rules adopted on the international level. Otherwise, national sport federations could suffer disciplinary sanctions from international sport federations, in the worst case even the loss of membership in international sport federation. The logic and regulation is hence the same as already described for OCS above.

54. National sport federations adopt the rules that have to be followed by sport clubs, but on the other hand national sport federations must also follow rules adopted either by national (e.g., OCS) and international (e.g., UEFA, FIFA, FIS, IOC) sport associations if they are or wish to become their members. Therefore, their independence is quite relative. Inter-municipal sport federations are even more dependent since they are members of national sport organizations and must therefore follow the rules of national sport federations.

55. The structure of bodies established in federations and associations also usually follows the same principle as described above in the OCS chapter. The main reason is that these federations and associations are established according to the Societies Act. Each legal person that is established as a society according to the Societies Act, must at least form a General Assembly and appoint a legal representative, all other bodies are optional. As it is not operationally effective that all decisions are made by a General Assembly, societies usually form other bodies, such as Executive Committee, Supervisory Board and Disciplinary Commission.[43] Small societies sometimes do not form such bodies, but federations and associations always do.

A. Slovenian Football Association

56. Articles of Association[44] of Slovenian Football Association state that its members are nine inter-municipal football federations[45] and two professional organizations: The Association of Slovenian Football Referees and The Association of Slovenian Football Coaches (Article 10). Members must comply with the rules set by Slovenian Football Association and ensure that the articles of association of their members are in accordance with the articles of association of Slovenian Football Association.

57. Articles of Associations of nine inter-municipal football federations state that their members can be football clubs that are operating in an area covered by a specific inter-municipal football federation if they accept their rules. Some inter-municipal football federations allow that their members can also be local associations of football coaches and referees.

---

43. V. Kokalj, *Zakon o društvih s komentarjem*, 69–72, 94 (GV Založba, Ljubljana).
44. Available only in Slovenian language at: https://www.nzs.si/Doc/1.0_Statut%20NZS_V3.0_%C4%8Distopis_25042019_final.pdf (accessed 3 Aug. 2019).
45. Celje, Gorenjska, Lendava, Ljubljana, Koper, Maribor, Murska Sobota, Nova Gorica and Ptuj.

58. Although football clubs are not directly members of the Slovenian Football Association, the Football Association of Slovenia according to regulations on the registration and enrolment of football clubs[46] keeps a registration of all football clubs that are indirectly its members.

59. Slovenian Football Association probably has the most professional and developed structure of bodies. This fact is closely connected to the amount of funds it has in the budget. These funds are by far the biggest among sport federations and associations in Slovenia. According to Articles of Association the following (eight) governing bodies are established in Slovenian Football Association:

- General Assembly is the highest authority. Delegates represent every inter-municipal football federation who is a member of the federation. The number of delegates who represent it depends on the number of members that inter-municipal football federation has. Association of football referees and coaches each have two delegates. Each delegate has one vote, except in certain specific decisions (e.g., adopting and amending the articles of association) when each member has one vote. General Assembly renders the most important decisions (e.g., adopting and amending the articles of association, elects and dismisses the president, the arbitration council members and the Supervisory Board members).
- Executive Committee is an executive body that has seventeen members: the president four vice-presidents and twelve other members (eleven presidents of the above-mentioned members and the president of association of first league clubs). The tasks of the Executive Committee are, e.g., executes the decisions of the General Assembly, appoints and dismisses the Secretary-General, decides on the purchase and sale of real estate, decides on colour combinations of national team jerseys and equipment.
- Arbitration Council has five members. The decisions are rendered in a panel of three members. The competence of the Arbitration Council is to make last instance decisions: (1) on disputes between members of the Slovenian Football Associations and between members of the Slovenian Football Association and the Slovenian Football Association arising from the relationships governed by the Slovenian Football Association's regulations, and (2) on other matters, if required by the Slovenian Football Association's regulations. The decisions of the Arbitration Council are final, except decisions on exclusion and suspension of membership rights when General Assembly makes a final decision.
- Supervisory Board consists of five members. Its main assignment is to control the legality and cost-effective operation of the Slovenian Football Association.
- President of Slovenian Football Association is its legal representative. He has mostly operational task: chairs the General Assembly meeting, convenes and chairs meetings of the Executive Board, suggests team selectors etc. Four Vice-Presidents assist him. They are in charge of specific areas, e.g., finance and marketing, international affairs, youth football.

---

46. Available only in Slovenian language at: https://www.nzs.si/Doc/Arhiv/Predpisi%20NZS/03a_Pravilnik_o_registraciji_in_vpisu_nogometnih_klubov_v_register_NZS_V1_0_30112011.pdf (accessed 3 Aug. 2019).

- Secretary-General of Slovenian Football Association is the chief operating officer. Besides the President, he also legally represents the Association and is the head of professional services (accounting, human resources).
- Committee on urgent matters consists of the President and Vice-Presidents. This Committee decides on urgent matters between two meetings of the Executive Board. All those decisions for which Executive Board is competent, that need to be made immediately and the Executive Board meeting cannot be called in time, are urgent matters. Committee on urgent matters must inform the Executive Board at its first meeting of the decisions and ask their approval.
- First Instance and Appeal Bodies have the competence to decide independently at the first and second instance on competition matters, registration matters, disciplinary matter and licensing matters.

B. Slovenian Ski Association

60. Slovenian Ski Association is an association of different ski branches: alpine skiing, ski jumping, Nordic combination, cross-country skiing, biathlon, freestyle skiing, snowboarding, telemark skiing and skiing of persons with disabilities. According to the Articles of Association of the Slovenian Ski Association,[47] (ski) clubs are its direct members (Article 10). By becoming members of a national federation, ski clubs oblige to follow its rules. Despite the direct membership of (ski) clubs in Slovenian Ski Association, Articles of Association allow (ski) clubs to associate on a regional level with other (ski) clubs if they wish to. This does not affect their direct membership with Slovenian Ski Association, as regional associations cannot become its members.

61. According to its Articles of Association Slovenian Ski Association has five governing bodies:

- General Assembly, which is the highest authority, composed of (regular) members represented by representatives. Their right to vote depends on several factors (number of members, performance of members and organization of competitions). Members who are more successful according to these criteria have more votes. General Assembly makes the most important decisions (e.g., adopts Articles of Association, elects and dismisses the president of Association, decides on termination of membership).
- Executive Committee is a governing body that makes major decisions that are not within the competence of the General Assembly (e.g., approves the business plan, considers the annual report). Executive Committee is a collegiate body composed of President and two vice-presidents of Association, presidents of the ski industries, president of society of coaches and teachers of skiing, representatives

47. Available only in Slovenian language at: https://www.sloski.si/resources/files/pdf/Zveza/17_18/Statut_veljavni_na_dan_27_12_2017.pdf (accessed 3 Aug. 2019).

of the Association that are members of the FIS or International Biathlon Union (IBU) board and a representative of organizing committees for the World Cup competitions in Slovenia.
- President of Association is a representative of the Association. He has to implement decisions of the General Assembly and Executive Committee and is responsible for the legality of the operation of the Association. His main task is conducting ongoing day-to-day business. He is the head of professional services (accounting, human resources etc.).
- Supervisory Board has five members, and its main task is to control the legality and cost-effective operation of the Slovenian Ski Association.
- Honorary Tribunal is a body that conducts proceedings and pronounces penalties in case of violations of the rules of the Association.

IV. Sport Clubs

62. Sport clubs are members of sport federations. They can be direct members of national sport federations or this connection is indirect through inter-municipal sport federations. Sport clubs are not direct members of OCS, but only through sport federations. As (direct or indirect) members, sport clubs must comply with not only public regulation but also private regulation set by OCS, sport federations and associations. Membership enables them to compete on a national and international level, as it is the minimal condition for taking part in competition. Sport federations often set additional conditions for taking part in competitions, especially on higher levels.

A. Legal Status

63. Although it is theoretically possible for sport clubs to operate informally, that is without being legal entities, this is not practical. Besides that, Societies Act and autonomous private regulation in Slovenia prevent unincorporated associations from being members of (sports) federations. Therefore, in practise none of the competing sport clubs is without legal personality. That is the reason why we will not deal with unincorporated associations in this monograph.[48]

64. There are many forms of legal entities in Slovenian legislation.[49] Sport clubs could, at least in theory, operate in forms like cooperative, foundation, private institute, but that would not be very appropriate. Besides the form of incorporated associations (societies), sport clubs could easily operate as companies, especially as Limited Liability Companies or as Joint Stock Companies,[50] but Slovenian public regulation (the Societies Act) together with autonomous private regulation do not

48. A brief analysis on this topic can be found in J. Podlipnik, *Pravni in davčni status športnih klubov*, 85–88 (PhD Thesis, Law faculty in Ljubljana 2010).
49. For a complete review of different forms, *see* V. Trstenjak, *Pravne osebe* (GV Založba 2003).
50. J. Podlipnik, *Pravni in davčni status športnih klubov*, 89–114 (PhD Thesis, Law faculty in Ljubljana 2010).

allow that. Two legal forms are discussed in this monograph: societies and companies. But before that it should be emphasized that all sport clubs are, by legal form, societies. If it is allowed by sport federation, sport clubs can establish a company and exercise its competitive rights through it. It has been argued that a current legal regime that does not enable forming (at least professional) sport clubs as companies is spent out.[51] We agree with this position, but believe that some limitations, especially regarding distribution of profits should still remain, set by either public or private regulation.[52] So it would be advisable that special form of Sport Company should be introduced in the Slovenian legal system. On occasion debates of this kind appear in the public, but the Government has not yet prepared any official document that would suggest such change.

1. Sport Clubs as Societies

65. All sport clubs in Slovenia are incorporated societies according to the Societies Act. The society is an independent and non-profit association formed by the founders to pursue their common interests. The society is a legal entity. The purpose of the establishment and operation of a society must not be gaining profit. This does not mean that societies must not engage in economic (for profit) activities, but merely that economic activity must be connected to society's non-profit aims and objectives and that all profits (excess of revenue over expenses) must be used for the (non-profit) aims and objectives of the society and cannot be divided among its members.

66. Societies are corporations. This means that members are essential for forming a society. According to the Societies Act a minimum of three individuals (natural persons) with complete legal capacity or legal persons can establish a society. To establish a sport club, their common interest should be to practise sports and to compete in sport competitions.

67. Competent authority for the registration of societies is an administrative unit where the headquarters of the society is located. Societies are therefore not listed in court registry but rather in registry which is kept by public administration.

68. At least two societies are allowed to establish federation (association) of societies. In fact a federation of societies is a special form of society whose members can only be societies.[53] Since federations are special forms of associations, they can form and become a member of a higher federation, etc. This regulation is the

51. M. Ilešič, *Družbeni in pravni vidiki športa*, 45 (V. Bergant Rakočević ed., *Šport & pravo*, GV Založba 2008).
52. J. Podlipnik, *Pravni in davčni status športnih klubov*, 336 (PhD Thesis, Law faculty in Ljubljana 2010) and M. Ilešič, *Družbeni in pravni vidiki športa*, 45 (V. Bergant Rakočević ed., *Šport & pravo*, GV Založba 2008).
53. J. Podlipnik, *Pravni in davčni status športnih klubov*, 57 (PhD Thesis, Law faculty in Ljubljana 2010).

reason why all sport clubs in Slovenia are societies. No other legal form can become a member of federation or federation of federations.

2. Sport Clubs as Companies

69. More about this possibility is written later on in a section where private regulation of Slovenian Football Association is described. At this point, I would just like to emphasize that in some sports, autonomous rules allow sport societies that have the licence (right) to compete to transfer the exercise of their licence to some forms of companies which they establish and in which they have at least the prescribed majority of votes. The licence therefore still remains in the hands of a club, and the club stays completely responsible for the legality of operation of its company.

70. This means that in Slovenia sport clubs cannot (yet) operate as companies, but they can execute certain competing rights through companies, which they establish in order to compete. This possibility is only possible if rules of the national sport federations (association) allow the transfer of the execution of licence.

71. Usually only limited liability companies and joint stock companies are appropriate for this task. The court is competent for the registration of the companies. These companies are 'ordinary' companies without any sport peculiarities, but as we will see below, autonomous rules of sport organizations usually demand that sport clubs, if these companies are established with third persons, keep at least the prescribed majority of voting rights.

B. Membership in Sport Federations and Associations

72. Sport clubs are either direct or indirect (through regional sport federations) members of sport federations. It is customary that sport federations maintain a register of sport clubs that are competing in competitions organized by sport federations. With registration within certain sport federation (association) sport clubs submit to the rules of regional and national sport federations and also to the rules of national (e.g., OCS) and international sports organizations (e.g., UEFA, FIFA, FIS), that such sport federation is a member on an international level.

73. Registration of the club within national sport federation is a prerequisite for participating in competitions organized by such sport federations. Usually sport clubs only have to fulfil some basic conditions to be able to register, such as legal entity under the Societies Act, involvement in sport discipline that sport federation is involved in, certain number of competitors who are registered for sport club, payment of membership fee to sport federation, statements to comply with rules of sport federation and rules of sport federations that this sport federation is a member of, etc.

74. In some cases sport clubs must accept additional obligations if they wish to compete in higher levels of competition. They must acquire a licence to compete. This licence is also granted by sport federations. Licences are customary in team (collective) sports. In order to acquire a licence sport clubs must meet different criteria, such as sporting criteria, infrastructure criteria, staff and administrative criteria, legal criteria, financial criteria, and so on. Without a licence, a sport club cannot compete on national (usually only higher levels of competition) and international level.

1. Slovenian Football Association

a. Registration of Clubs

75. Rules on the registration and enrolment of football clubs in the Slovenian Football Association's register[54] state that all football clubs established in Slovenia that wish to become members of Slovenian Football Association need to be registered with this sport federation. Without membership, clubs cannot compete in competitions organized by this sport federation. A special registration procedure is laid down by these rules. In order to be registered, football club needs to file an application to register to which it must attach these written statements and documents that must not be older than three months:

- a statement in which it undertakes to fully comply with the statutes, regulations, instructions and decisions of FIFA, UEFA, the Slovenian Football Association and inter-municipal football associations (federations), the FIFA Code of Ethics, and to ensure that club's officials and players will also comply with them;
- a statement to abide by the principles of loyalty, integrity and sportsmanship in accordance with the principles of fair play;
- a statement that the club will comply with the applicable rules football game, set by the International Football Association Board (IFAB), or rules of the game laid down by FIFA, for beach football (beasal) and hall football (futsal);
- a statement that it will play all the official home matches in Slovenia, except in cases provided for by the rules of UEFA and FIFA;
- a statement that it will organize international friendly matches in accordance with the rules of the Slovenian Football Association, UEFA and FIFA;
- a statement that it recognizes the jurisdiction and decisions of football arbitration and Court of Arbitration for Sport (CAS);
- a statement that the club will at first try to solve all disputes relating to sport competition with the Slovenian Football Association, UEFA or FIFA, and that the club agrees with the exclusion of the jurisdiction of the ordinary courts if this is allowed by the Slovenian public order;

54. Available only in Slovenian language at: https://www.nzs.si/Doc/Arhiv/Predpisi%20NZS/03a_Pravilnik_o_registraciji_in_vpisu_nogometnih_klubov_v_register_NZS_V1_0_30112011.pdf (accessed 4 Aug. 2019).

- a statement that it has no sports relations with entities unrecognized by Slovenian Football Association, UEFA and FIFA or by those persons who are outlawed or suspended by Slovenian Football Association, UEFA or FIFA;
- a statement that it agrees with the publication of data in the registry and that it is aware that third persons will have access to the register in accordance with these rules;
- a statement that submitted statements and documents are accurate and perfect;
- an extract from the public registry showing that it is a legal entity registered with the competent Slovenian authority;
- minutes of the founding of the Assembly and the list of founders;
- a valid copy of the articles of association and the other valid rules;
- a list of legal and statutory representatives, and persons who have the authority to conclude binding legal acts with third parties, with the specimen signature of such persons;
- imprints of the official stamps;
- proof of payment of registration fees or membership fees; and
- proof of applying for registration of a minimum number of football players (fifteen for ordinary football or ten for small football).

b. Licensing of Clubs

76. Articles of Association of the Slovenian Football Association state in Article 49 that football clubs have to have a licence in order to participate in competitions organized by either Slovenian Football Association or UEFA competitions. Licence can only be acquired by registered football clubs; besides that, minimum registration periods are prescribed.[55] Slovenian Football Association issues licence to clubs. Clubs must acquire licences every year for competing in UEFA competitions and for competing in three highest Slovenian leagues. Slovenian Football Association has comprehensive rules about clubs' licensing. Rules for licensing football clubs[56] prescribe competence for issuing a licence, licensing procedure, legal remedies against the decision and conditions for obtaining a licence. In this monograph, we will only shortly deal with groups of conditions for obtaining a licence.

77. Before we shortly present groups of licence conditions, it must be noted that not all licence conditions must necessarily be met. Rules divide the conditions into three groups. In Group A are conditions without which licence for competing on certain level of competition cannot be granted. If a football club does not fulfil Group B conditions, it can still acquire a licence to compete in certain level of competition, but with disciplinary penalty. Group C conditions are only recommendations and are therefore not mandatory. No sanctions arise if a club does not meet these.

55. For UEFA and first Slovenian football league licence, clubs have to be registered at least three consecutive years, for second Slovenian football league licence they have to be registered for at least two consecutive years and for third Slovenian football league licence one-year registration is required. One-year period is also sufficient for the first Women Slovenian Football League licence.
56. Available only in Slovenian language at: https://www.nzs.si/Doc/Info/2018/Pravilnik%20o%20licenciranju%20nogometnih%20klubov_V6.0.pdf (accessed 4 Aug. 2019).

78. Licence is only needed for competing in international UEFA competitions, national highest three Slovenian league competitions for men and the highest (first) Slovenian Women Football League. In other competitions, clubs can compete without acquiring licences. Conditions for obtaining a licence for UEFA competitions are the most stringent, and then they lower with the level of competition.

79. Licence conditions are divided into five groups:

(1) Sports – football schools, junior teams must compete in certain levels of competition, certain number of junior competitors, healthcare for football players must be guaranteed, members of staff must be sent to different educational seminars, club must promote fair play and non-discrimination among his players and staff.
(2) Infrastructure – a club must own or lease a proper stadium and training infrastructure.
(3) Staff and administration – a club must have a contract concluded with general manager, general secretary, financial manager, head of security, security service, a person responsible for public relations, a person responsible for fans, a doctor, physiotherapist, head coach, assistant coach, head of junior programme, coaches for junior teams.
(4) Legal:
  (a) The club must state in writing that:
    – it will comply with the statutes, regulations, directives and decisions of FIFA, UEFA and the Slovenian Football Association and all disputes will be resolved before CAS;
    – it will participate exclusively in official competitions of the Slovenian Football Association;
    – it will participate exclusively in international UEFA and FIFA competitions (provision does not apply to friendly matches);
    – it will notify in writing Slovenian Football Association of any change regarding conditions for acquiring a licence;
    – it will respect the terms and conditions set out in the Rules for licensing football clubs of Slovenian Football Association and UEFA Rules for licensing clubs and financial Fair Play;
    – all submitted documents are complete and accurate;
    – Slovenian Football Association, UEFA and CAS have the power to view or obtain and document information from the competent private and public bodies;
    – it recognizes the right of UEFA to conduct random compliance audits; and
    – its representatives will respect the confidentiality and secrecy of data and other information, which they received from the licensing authorities of the Slovenian Football Association, if a written agreement is not specified otherwise.
  (b) The club must submit the following documents:
    – a copy of its valid articles of association;
    – the original extract from the public register.

(5) Financial – a club must prepare and sometimes also audit financial statements, the club must describe in writing if any financial changes occurred from the date of his financial statement, the club must show in writing that it will be able to do business at least until the end of the licensing season, and the club must prove that it has no financial liabilities:
   (a) that result from transfer of football players;
   (b) to employees, dependent persons, social security contributions, taxes and other public duties.

80. As it was mentioned above, clubs that acquire a licence have the right to compete by themselves or they can establish a dependent company in which they have at least a prescribed majority of voting rights and compete with this legal entity. To compete with a company, club must have a contract concluded with such a company, and this contract must be approved by the Slovenian Football Association. Such a contract must have the following minimum content:

- the associated legal entity must state that it will fully comply with the valid statutes, regulations and other regulations and decisions of FIFA, UEFA and the Slovenian Football Association;
- the associated legal person must bind not to transfer licensing rights arising from a contract with the club (including the right to participate in national and international competitions);
- that associated legal persons are aware that its right to participate in national and international competitions will cease to exist if the club loses its membership in Slovenian Football Association;
- that if a process of bankruptcy or liquidation will begin against the club, the licence cannot be transferred;
- that, if the process of bankruptcy or liquidation will begin against associated legal person, licence will immediately be withdrawn;
- that the Slovenian Football Association has the right to approve the names of the competing teams in national and international competitions;
- that on the request of the CAS associated legal person will provide all documents and information on matters relating to its activities in connection with the participation of teams national and international competitions;
- that the club has at least 26%[57] of the voting rights in an associated legal person and associated legal person is not directly or indirectly owned or operated by anyone who has decisive influence in another registered member or its associated entity; and
- that not only the contract but also any amendment or modification of this contract shall become effective after approval by the Slovenian Football Association.

---

57. Previous rules demanded that clubs should have more than half (50%) of voting rights. The mandatory percentage probably dropped to attract private investors. By lowering the percentage, private investors can indirectly enter the ownership of sport clubs.

2. Slovenian Ski Association

a. Registration of Clubs

81. In order for sport club to register and therefore become a member of Slovenian Ski Association it has to (Article 11 of Articles of Association of Slovenian Ski Association and Regulations on membership and voting rights[58]):

- file an application for membership declaring to follow the Articles of Association the same way as existing members;
- has to be a society according to the Societies Act;
- its rules must not be contrary to Articles of Association of Slovenian Ski Association;
- it has no outstanding financial and other liabilities to the Slovenian Ski Association that are already due; and
- the Honorary Tribunal did not suspend its regular membership rights.

b. Licensing of Clubs

82. Slovenian Ski Association does not regulate licensing of clubs.

58. Available only in Slovenian language at: https://www.sloski.si/resources/files/pdf/Zveza/18_19/Pravilnik_o_clanstvu_in_glasovalnih_pravicah_SZS_5_6_2019.pdf (accessed 4 Aug. 2019).

Chapter 2. Public Regulation

§1. Fundamental Rights and Other Constitutional Provisions

I. Freedom of Assembly and Association (Article 42)

83. According to Article 42 of the Constitution everyone has the right to associate freely with others. Legal restrictions of this right are permissible where so required for national security or public safety and for protection against the spread of infectious diseases. The freedom of association is a fundamental human freedom protected by the Constitution. Although only three legal restrictions to this freedom are expressly stated in Article 42, I must note that Article 15 of the Constitution states that human rights and fundamental freedoms are not absolute[59] and can also be limited by other constitutionally protected human rights and fundamental freedoms of others (equality before the law, protection of human personality and dignity, right to judicial protection, etc.). The limitations must also be proportionate (Article 2 of the Constitution).

84. Barring the above-mentioned restrictions (physical and legal)[60] persons are free to associate in order to achieve their objectives or interests. This includes sportive objectives and interests. According to the jurisprudence of the Slovenian Constitutional Court,[61] the freedom of association can be exercised informally or formally. Persons associate informally when they pursue to achieve their objectives and interest through unincorporated associations (without establishing a legal entity).[62] If they wish to associate formally, they are generally free to choose among different legal forms provided in a legal system (a so-called *numerus clausus* principle). The most important legal consequence of a formal association is that the law recognizes the forms of organized association and the rights and duties arising thereof (legal capacity). However, in case of formal associations, persons have to comply with the rules that the law provides for the establishment and operation of such legal form.

85. Although they are theoretically possible, informal unincorporated associations have practical disadvantages regarding their liability, representation, stability, etc. These are the reasons why legal personality is one of the basic conditions for joining sport federations. In practice all sport associations and sport federations are legal entities.

59. K. Vatovec, *A Commentary of the Article 15*, 411 (M. Avbelj ed., *Komentar Ustave Republike Slovenije*, Part I, Nova univerza, Evropska pravna fakulteta 2019).
60. L. Šturm, *Komentar Ustave Republike Slovenije*, 462 (L. Šturm ed., Fakulteta za državne in evropske študije 2010).
61. Decision of Constitutional Court of Republic of Slovenia U-I-155/07 of 9 Apr. 2009.
62. This is actually a partnership contract between members and the Arts 990–1002 of Code of Obligations (Official Journal of the Republic of Slovenia, No. 97/07) would apply.

86. This constitutional provision allows establishment and operation of sport clubs, sport federations and OCS[63] as legal entities. In general, there are no constitutional mandates that would require a sport organization to be established in a certain legal form(s). Sporting organizations could therefore theoretically be established in any of the forms allowed by Slovenian legislation according to the *numerus clausus* principle (associations, companies, institutions, cooperatives, foundations, etc.).[64] However, certain public acts and especially private regulation prescribe restrictions, so that currently all sport clubs and sport federations in Slovenia are non-profit societies. The pyramid structure is therefore not the consequence of constitutional provisions but rather of the so-called European Model of Sport.

II. Free Enterprise (Article 74)

87. Famous sport clubs (FC Barcelona, Manchester United, etc.), athletes (Cristiano Ronaldo, Lionel Messi, etc.) are proof that competing in sport can be a great business. Free enterprise in Article 74 of the Constitution, in principle, not only guarantees free economic initiative but also sets some limitations to this freedom. The first and the most important one for this monograph is that the law sets conditions for establishing commercial organizations. This limitation is similar to the one that I already mentioned above when discussing the content of Article 42 (Freedom of Association), except that this one is narrower and is only applicable to potential business association. Natural and legal persons are only allowed to establish commercial organizations that are prescribed by the law (*numerus clausus* principle). However, this does not mean that non-profit associations covered by Article 42 are prohibited from conducting any business, but some limitations are set to them by the law (their sole purpose must not be doing business, they must not divide the realized profit, etc.).

88. Two other limitations to freedom of entrepreneurship exist that are not essential for this monograph. The first one prohibits commercial activities to be pursued in a manner contrary to public interest, and the second prohibits unfair competition practices and practices, which restrict competition in a manner contrary to the law.

III. Protection of Right to Privacy and Personality Rights (Article 35)

89. Article 35 of the Slovenian Constitution states that inviolability of the physical and mental integrity of every person, his privacy and personality rights is guaranteed. According to the jurisprudence of the Slovenian Constitutional Court[65] this

63. J. Tratnik, *Pregled pozitivno pravne zakonodaje, ki ureja šport*, 5 (M. Ilešič & T. Jagodic eds, Olimpijski komite Slovenije 1994).
64. M. Ilešič, *Pravni status športnih organizacij*, Podjetje in delo, 6-7/2005, 1642–1643.
65. Decisions of the Slovenian Constitutional Court, Nos U-I-202/93 of 6 Oct. 1994, U-I-283/99 of 20 Mar. 2003 and U-I-218/07 of 26 Mar. 2009.

human right also protects so-called general freedom to act. An element of this freedom is also the principle of autonomy in contractual law. This constitutional provision also protects personality rights that are very important commercial goods of top athletes.[66]

IV. Taxes (Article 147)

90. Article 147 is basically a special principle of legality in the field of taxation.[67] Only the Parliament is allowed to impose taxes, customs duties and other charges only by law. Therefore, as the Government is not competent to adopt laws, it is not allowed to impose taxes, customs and other duties. Local communities are only allowed to impose taxes and other charges under conditions provided by the Constitution and law. This constitutional provision does not give the legislator absolute discretion in prescribing taxes. He is bound to other constitutional provisions that do not expressly mention taxes but limit the legislator (e.g., right to private property and inheritance, right to personal dignity and safety, equality before the law).[68]

§2. Governmental Conditions and Permits

91. Slovenia prescribes governmental conditions and permits mostly in connection to performance of work. It is usually not important what is the legal status (employed person, entrepreneur) of the person that performs the work. Otherwise, Slovenia does not prescribe permits for the establishment of legal entities. A legal entity may be established as soon as the prescribed conditions are met.

I. Employment Relationships Act

92. According to Articles 211 and 212 of the Employment Relationships Act,[69] children under 15 years old are not allowed to work. This general restriction is not limited to employment relationships.[70] A child under the age of 15 may exceptionally, for a fee, participate in *inter alia* the preparation and performance of artistic, scenic and other works in the field of sports. This does not mean that children under the age of 15 can compete in return for remuneration. The law targets different participation (e.g., wiping the floor at basketball games). This restriction, which is

66. More about constitutional issues of personality rights, *see* P. Farmany, *Komentar Ustave Republike Slovenije*, Part I, 339–349 (M. Avbelj ed., Nova univerza, Evropska pravna fakulteta 2019).
67. Decision of Slovenian Constitutional Court, Nos U-I-215/11, Up-1128/11, of 10 Jan. 2013.
68. More about these limitations in Slovenian legal order, *see* J. Podlipnik, *Komentar Ustave Republike Slovenije*, Part I, 651–660 (M. Avbelj ed., Nova univerza, Evropska pravna fakulteta 2019).
69. Official Journal of Slovenia, Nos 21/13, 78/13, 47/15, 33/16, 52/16, 15/17 and 22/19.
70. M. Šetinc Tekavc, *Zakon o delovnih razmerjih s komentarjem*, 1106 (N. Belopavlovič, B. Kresal, K. Kresal Šoltes & D. Senčur Peček eds, IUS Software 2016).

based on international treaties signed by Slovenia,[71] and EU Directives,[72] causes that one cannot register as a professional athlete before the age of 15.

II. Health and Safety at Work Act

93. Health and Safety Work Act establishes the rights and duties of employers and workers in relation to safe and healthy work and measures to ensure safety and health at work.[73] Its provisions apply in all activities to all persons present in the work process. The terms 'worker' and 'employer' under this Act are wide. It covers not only persons who concluded an employment contract but also anyone who performs work (worker) for the other person (employer), unless otherwise provided by law. Exemptions for sport are not prescribed. The provisions of this Act and other regulations on safety and health at work also apply to self-employed persons. They are responsible for their own safety and health and for the safety and health of others affected by their actions or omissions.

94. I will not go into detailed presentation of the content of this Act. Its basic principle is that employers must ensure the safety and health of workers at work. To this end, they must take measures necessary to ensure the safety and health of workers and other persons present in the work process, including the prevention, elimination and management of occupational hazards, information and training of workers, with appropriate organization and the necessary material resources. Workers must:

- respect and implement measures to ensure safety and health at work;
- perform their work with such care that they protect their life and health and that of other persons; and
- use the means of work, safety devices and personal protective equipment according to their purpose and the instructions of employers, carefully handle them and ensure that they are in perfect condition.

95. The obligations under Health and Safety at Work Act are financially quite burdensome for the employers and self-employed persons. Not all of them are aware of the duties they have. Different inspectorates carry out the enforcement of the Act. In the case of violations, they may fine the offenders.

71. International Labour Organization, Minimum Age Convention, 1973 (No. 138).
72. Council Directive 94/33/EC of 22 June 1994 on the protection of young people at work, amended with a Directive 2007/30/EC of the European Parliament and of the Council of 20 June 2007 and Directive 2014/27/EU of the European Parliament and of the Council of 26 February 2014.
73. Official Journal of Slovenia, No. 43/11.

III. Employment, Self-Employment and Work of Foreigners Act

96. Employment, Self-Employment and Work of Foreigners Act determines the conditions for employment, self-employment and work of foreigners and the related tasks of the Republic of Slovenia for regulating and protecting the labour market.[74] According to this Act, a foreigner is everyone without Slovenian citizenship, but the provisions of the Act also do not apply to citizens of other EU Member States (free movement of workers as one of the four freedoms enjoyed by EU citizens). Besides, the Act enacts a few other exceptions, one of them is also important for this monograph. Foreign workers and self-employed persons, who fall under the provisions of the Act, must obtain a permit in order to work in Slovenia. They acquire the right to work only if it is first established that there are no suitable persons listed in in the unemployment register. Regarding the working quotas, the Act states that the Government can allot them, but currently there is none.

97. According to Article 5.2(14) the provisions of this Act do not apply to foreigners who meet all of the following conditions:

- who are professional athletes (sportsmen) or private sports workers under the Sports Act;[75]
- who have concluded a cooperation agreement with a Slovenian club or sports organization established in the Republic of Slovenia; and
- who are registered as professional athletes (sportsmen) or private sports workers, within ninety days from the date of the first entered into the Republic of Slovenia.

98. The intent of the legislator is quite clear. Working in sport is specific, and applying regular provisions that apply to other sectors would be inappropriate. However, the legal formulation of the provision has its faults. According to Article 62 of the Sports Act private sports workers and professional athletes are by definition those who perform their work independently. Technically those professional athletes and private sports workers who perform their work in the employment relationship cannot be independent, so they could not acquire the needed status. Hence, the legislator should reformulate the provision.

IV. Sports Act

99. According to Sports Act (Articles 46–58) professional work in sport involves planning, organization, implementation, monitoring and assessment of the process of the sports practice, teaching of individuals and courses in sports that are registered under the official competition system. Not just anyone can perform such work. Workers must be sufficiently qualified.

---

74. Official Journal of Slovenia, Nos 1/18 (Official Consolidated Text) and 31/18.

75. More about the statuses of professional athlete (sportsman) and private sports worker, *see below*, Part II. Sports and Employment.

100. The Act states that professional work can only be carried out by a professional who:

- has appropriate professional education or professional qualifications in accordance with this Act;
- is registered as a worker with professional education and qualifications in sports;
- (in certain cases) has not been finally convicted of a wilful offence prosecuted ex officio and sentenced to unconditional imprisonment for more than six months or has not been finally convicted for committing a criminal offence against sexual inviolability; and
- who knows Slovenian when working with children, unless translation is provided.

101. Appropriate professionally educated is a person holding a degree in the relevant field of sport in accordance with the criteria laid down by the Minister. Those who do not have such a degree can gain professional qualifications if:

- they are at least 18 years old;
- have at least a prescribed level of education; and
- have a first or second degree professional qualification in sports training, sports recreation, sports practice of people with disabilities or elderly people under officially recognized training programmes in accordance with this Act.[76]

§3. Tort Law (Civil Law Liability)

102. Sport is useful, but at the same time, it can be dangerous. Physical activity and the involvement of several people can lead to accidents and injuries. Liability for damages can arise in different situations: responsibility of organizers of sporting events, liability of athletes, etc.[77] 'The role of the law of tort is to compensate those who have suffered loss as a result of the fault of another.'[78] Below, I address only some general issues and the tortious (non-contractual) liability of athletes. These are the most typical examples of responsibility in sports.

I. General Issues

103. The fundamental principle of tort law is that the harm suffered by the person who caused it (Latin *Causam sentit dominus*).[79] This is also true in sports.[80]

76. The Act determines the scope of these programmes, and the Minister competent for sports determines the details with the assistance of experts. After completing the training, the person obtains a degree.
77. D. Možina, *Odškodninska odgovornost za poškodbe pri športu*, 273 (V. Bergant Rakočević ed., *Šport & pravo*, GV Založba 2008).
78. S. Gardiner, *Sport Law*, 629 (3rd ed., Cavendish Publishing Limited 2011).
79. D. Možina, *Odškodninska odgovornost za poškodbe pri športu*, 274 (V. Bergant Rakočević ed., *Šport & pravo*, GV Založba 2008).

Liability for damages arises if the following conditions of liability for damages set in the general Code of Obligations[81] are met:[82]

- Damage. The first condition for liability for damages is the occurrence of damage. This may be property damage or non-pecuniary damage. There are two forms of property damage: actual damage (loss of property) and loss of profit (preventing property increase). In the case of non-pecuniary damage, Slovenian law is recognized only if it involves any form of legally recognized damage: physical pain, mental anguish, fear, damage to the reputation of a legal person and loss of annual leave.
- Causal link. The cause of the damage must be the conduct or omission of the person causing the damage.
- Unlawfulness. The conduct of liability for damages must be contrary to legal norms or in an inadmissible manner interfere with legally protected interests. There are generally two concepts: wrongfulness of consequence and wrongfulness of conduct. In the field of sport, the concept of unlawful conduct is of particular relevance. The rules of conduct for athletes are adopted by sports organizations. It is often difficult to determine the boundary between slightly more brutal (but not prohibited) conduct and prohibited conduct. However, participants should be aware that they are subject to the general principle of care and avoidance of doing harm.[83]
- Culpable or strict liability. The basic form of liability in Slovenia is fault. The perpetrator is liable for damages if he acted intentionally or negligently. He negligently acts when he does otherwise than is expected of him. In the field of sports, we can speak of the standard of a caring athlete in a particular sport. Under Slovenian law, the perpetrator's fault is presumed, and he must prove that the damage occurred without his fault. Objective liability for damage is an exception and applies only in certain cases – if the damage originates from a dangerous thing or a dangerous activity. It should be noted that performing sports activities is not a mere activity in itself.[84] This is generally true of the damage caused by participants in a particular activity through joint action. Objective liability in sport can thus only be spoken of exceptionally when athletes would cause harm to third parties through the use of dangerous things (e.g., motorsport) or when a device operator (e.g., ski lifts) would cause harm to athletes.

80. F. Zeilner, *Sport und Recht*, 34–35 (Peter Lang 2003) and I. Crnić et al., *(Uvod u) športsko pravo*, 193 (Inženjerski biro 2009).
81. Official Journal of Slovenia, Nos 97/07 (Official Consolidated Text), 64/16 and 20/18.
82. D. Možina, *Odškodninska odgovornost za poškodbe pri športu*, 274–279 (V. Bergant Rakočević ed., *Šport & pravo*, GV Založba 2008).
83. Cf. I. Crnić et al., *(Uvod u) športsko pravo*, 205 (Inženjerski biro 2009).
84. Cf. N. Đurđević, *Osnov odgovornosti za štetu koju pretrpi sportista na sportskom takmičenju*, 757 (Zbornik radova Pravnog fakulteta u Splitu 4/2012).

II. Non-contractual (Tortious) Liability of Athletes

104. In general, it cannot be clearly stated when an athlete is liable for damages. His liability depends on the risk of the sports.[85] Legal theory[86] deals with different divisions of sports that affect risk.

105. The first criterion for division is the goal of a sports game. According to it, there are two groups of sports:

- So-called parallel sports – sports where the goal is to perform a task as quickly or as efficiently as possible. These are, e.g., skiing, athletics, golf and ice-skating.
- So-called sports with elements of combat – sports that aim to defeat an opponent in direct combat. These are, e.g., boxing, football, ice hockey, basketball, volleyball.

In sports with combat elements, there is a greater risk of injury and damage, so athletes will be less entitled to compensation in this case. There are various risks within each of these groups, so I should mention two other divisions for a more accurate presentation.

106. The second criterion for division is the existence of physical contact during the duration of a sports game. From this perspective, legal theory distinguishes between non-contact sports and contact sports. Non-contact are sports where competitors are not on the sports field at the same time. Contact sports are further divided into:

- those whose goal is overpowering opponents in a direct body battle (e.g., boxing, karate, judo);
- those in which physical contact permitted and is part of the game, but with the aim of overcoming the opponent's body (e.g., football, handball, basketball, hockey); and
- those where the opponents are simultaneously on the court but the physical body contact is not part of the game (e.g., tennis, swimming, volleyball, running).

In contact sports, the risk of harm is greater than in non-contact sports. However, even within the contact sports group, the risk in sports where body contact is part of the game is greater than in sports where it is not.

107. The third division is related to sports equipment. Sports equipment, which is a necessary prerequisite for playing sports, can in itself be a hazard (i.e., dangerous thing) to competitors and other participants (e.g., motoring, motorcycling), but may not be of this nature. In the second case, the sports equipment may be completely safe (e.g., jogging, sport dancing) or may be dangerous in competition (e.g., ball sports, javelin throwing).

85. N. Plavšak, M. Juhart & R. Vrenčur, *Obligacijsko pravo – splošni del*, 540–543 (GV Založba 2009).
86. I. Crnić et al., *(Uvod u) športsko pravo*, 202 (Inženjerski biro 2009).

108. In relation to liability for damage, the principle of (Latin) *volenti non fit inuria* is also mentioned in sport. It is therefore a question of consent to accept the risk of injury. This consent may be given explicitly, but as a rule, it is given in a concluding manner. By agreeing to participate in sports, the person also agrees that he or she may be injured. It should be noted that consensus covers not only cases where sports rules are fully complied with but also their minor violations, which are commonplace. It is not possible to imagine that every ordinary offence in, e.g., football or basketball could be liable for damages. This could cause nobody to want to go into these sports anymore.

§4. Criminal Law Liability

109. Slovenian Criminal Code[87] does not have a specific sports offence, nonetheless mentions the word 'sport'. In Articles 186 and 187, it deals with doping offences that will be dealt with below, and in Article 296 it mentions hooliganism (spectator violence). This does not mean that athletes cannot be held responsible for committing crimes when they engage in sports. They can commit classic offences (e.g., personal injury, murder, homicide, involvement in an altercation). In this chapter I will deal with so-called participator violence. Some other criminal law issues will be discussed in the relevant chapters below (doping, public safety).

I. General Issues

110. A person's conduct is a crime if all these general (objective and subjective) elements are given: unlawfulness, danger, prescriptiveness in the law, enforcement conduct and guilt.[88] It would go beyond the purpose of this monograph, if I described all of them in detail. However, it is important to emphasize that the latter (the guilt) is given, if the offender is sane and acted intentionally or negligently. Additionally, the perpetrator can be punished for the criminal offence committed through negligence only if the law so determines. This means that that intent is a regular form of guilt that applies to all crimes, and negligence as a form of guilt can only be used if so prescribed. This is especially important for participant violence, where injuries often result from negligence.

111. Different criminal sanctions exist according to the Criminal Code: penalties, warning sanctions, security measures and educational measures. There are four different types of penalties: imprisonment, fine, prohibition of driving a motor vehicle and expulsion of a foreigner from the country.

87. Official Journal of Slovenia, Nos 50/12 (Official Consolidated Text), 6/16, 54/15, 38/16 and 27/17.
88. L. Selinšek, *Kazensko pravo*, 96 (GV Založba 2007).

II. Participator Violence

112. Participator violence extends only to injury-causing incidents that occur between co-participants during the course of the game. Obeying the rules is an integral part of playing any sport. Once all participants agree to be bound by the constitutive rules of the game, the contest can take place. In most cases, an accidental or unintentional rule violation will be punished adequately by the game's own disciplinary system. However, a player performing intentional rule violations cannot truly be said to be playing the game.[89]

113. However, compliance with sports rules does not guarantee that the offender will not be held liable for the crime, in the same way that their violation does not constitute an automatic criminal liability. Based on the fact that a competitor has complied with the rules of the game or not we can conclude on the level of culpability in criminal law. If he complied with the rules of the game, he probably did not intentionally want to commit a crime. Criminal offences may only be committed when the rules of sport are grossly violated or when the perpetrator uses a sporting activity to commit a crime.[90]

114. With respect to criminal liability, views on the consent of the injured party can also be found in the Slovenian criminal law literature.[91] Those who take part in a sporting event, give (at least a presumed) consent into injury. However, the condition for excluding the existence of a crime is that the injury occurred following the rules of the game.

115. No matter which view theoretically seems more convincing, both give the same result. The offender is not responsible for the crime.

§5. Gambling

I. General Issues

116. In Slovenia, the Gaming Act regulates gambling. Gambling under this Act is a game in which the participants have the same opportunity to win winnings for the payment of a certain amount and the outcome of the game is solely or largely dependent on chance or some uncertain event. According to its provisions, the organization of games of chance is the exclusive right of the Republic of Slovenia, unless otherwise provided by this Act. Gambling may only be organized on the basis of a permit or concession from the competent authority. An exception to this rule exists.

117. There are two groups of gambling according to the Act:

89. S. Gardiner et al., *Sports Law*, 593 (Cavendish Publishing Limited 2005).
90. L. Bavcon et al., *Kazensko pravo – splošni del*, 262–263 (Uradni list Republike Slovenije 2003).
91. L. Selinšek, *Kazensko pravo*, 135–136 (GV Založba 2007).

– Classic games of chance. These are numerous lotteries, lotteries with currently known winnings, lottery quizzes, raffles, lots, sports predictions, sports betting, raffles and other similar games.
– Special games of chance. These are games played by players against a casino or against each other at special gaming tables with balls, dice, cards, gambling boards or slot machines, and betting and other similar games in accordance with international standards (e.g., poker, roulette, dice games, bets).

118. Generally organizers of gambling must acquire a concession from the state, but the Gaming Act also enables certain organizers to acquire only state permits, but only if they organize classic game of chance occasionally. Only associations and non-profit humanitarian organizations established in the Republic of Slovenia designated by the Government have this option if their purpose is obtaining funds for financing activities determined by their general acts. Decree defining associations and non-profit humanitarian organizations, which may occasionally organize classic games and the assignment criteria for occasional organized classic games,[92] state that organizers must be associations with the status of a non-governmental organization acting in the public interest according to Non-Governmental Organizations Act[93] (Articles 6–14). The organizer may only hold a lottery, raffle or bingo once a year with one draw. The party may sell the lottery tickets for a maximum of sixty days.

119. Exceptionally other associations are allowed to organize bingo or raffles as part of their own one-day cultural or entertainment programme. Additional conditions that must be met are that the total value of lottery tickets does not exceed the amount determined by the Ministry for Finance (currently EUR 5,000)[94] and the value of the individual winnings does not exceed the amount from which the gambling tax must be paid (currently EUR 300).[95] In this case associations do not even need to acquire a permit, they just have to notify the body competent for internal affairs that such a game will be organized no later than eight days before the event.

II. Sports Specifics in the Gaming Act

120. Gaming Act provides special exemptions for sports event organizers. According to its Article 15 sporting competition organizers that fulfil general conditions for acquirement of a permit may once a year organize placing of bets on the venue where the competitions take place.

92. Official Journal of Slovenia, Nos 70/00 and 109/12.
93. Official Journal of Slovenia, No. 21/18.
94. Rules on classical games that can be organized without a licence (Official Journal, No. 14/09), Art. 2.
95. Taxation Act on Prizes from the Classical Games of Chance (Official Journal of Slovenia, No. 24/08) Art. 2.4.

121. Additional exception applies to organizers of these horse sporting (racing) competitions: harness racing, trot racing under saddle, straight gallop races and gallop races across obstacles. They may organize placing of bets in connection with these competitions up to twenty-five times a year if these competitions are organized according to the provisions of the Livestock Farming Act.[96] The organizer must obtain the consent of the minister responsible for agriculture for the organization of bets.

§6. Public Safety

I. General Issues

122. Public safety is closely linked to public sporting events. Sports Act has some definitions on such events, but provisions of other acts, mostly by Public Assembly Act,[97] regulate the main content.

123. Sports events are organized sports meetings and competitions (Article 72 of the Sports Act). A sports facility at the time of a sporting event is a sports facility where a sporting event takes place, from the entrance to the sports facility where the last ticket inspection is carried out or the organizer's measures are taken to prevent the introduction of dangerous objects and substances on the sports facility (Article 73 of the Sports Act).

124. Sporting events are often made available to anyone unconditionally or under certain conditions (e.g., purchase of a ticket). If so, they are public events according to the Public Assembly Act. Private sporting events are also possible, but I will ignore them in this monograph.

125. According to the Public Assembly Act, execution of a public event must be either previously notified to the competent authority (i.e., police) by the organizer or the organizer must beforehand acquire a permit from the administrative unit. Certain minor public events can be executed without a notification or a permit (Article 12). The Act states that permit must be issued:

- for an event on a public road, if they constitute extraordinary use of the road (e.g., bicycle race, marathon);
- for an international sporting event and membership competition in collective sports, if at least one club of the first national league participates in it;
- for an event that uses open flames or objects or devices that could endanger human life or property or property; and
- for an event with more than 3,000 participants expected.

96. Official Journal of Slovenia, Nos 18/02, 110/02, 45/04, 90/12 and 45/15.
97. Official Journal of Slovenia, No. 64/11 (Official Consolidated Text).

126. Before issuing the permit, the competent authority must verify that the organizer has envisaged sufficient measures to ensure order and safety at the event. If it finds that the measures are not sufficient, it may order the organizer to provide additional measures. The Act does not prescribe exhaustively what these measures are. The competent body chooses them according to the circumstances of the case. However, the choice must respect the principle of proportionality.[98]

II. Sports Specifics in the Public Assembly Act

127. The Act contains several sport specificities. With Article 9.2 the legislator ordered the Government to determine the general measures to be taken by the owners or operators of sports facilities and the organizers of sports events in these facilities to ensure order, safety of participants and other persons and property at events. Sporting events are specific public gatherings that require special measures.[99] This confirms the content of the European Convention on Spectator Violence and Misbehavior at Sports Events and in particular at Football Matches[100] which is signed and ratified by Slovenia. The Government adopted the decree on general measures applied to sport facilities during sports events[101] that provides e.g.:

- The organizer must ensure that banners with messages and labels that incite violence are not brought to the sports facility.
- The owner or organizer of the non-alcoholic beverage dispensing event must ensure that the beverages are only dispensed in plastic jars or other packaging that does not endanger participants.
- In the event of the expected arrival of an organized cheerleading group for which serious breaches of order or security are expected, the organizer must inform the competent police station and cooperate with the police throughout the event to ensure the order and safety of participants and other persons and property both at the event itself and in the venue.
- To maintain order at the event, the organizer must provide a sufficient number of safety stewards, the number of which must commensurate with the number of participants and their structure, risk of the event and other circumstances that could affect the safe course of the event.

128. The Act states that the competent body can order the organizer of a sporting event in a collective sports industry to obtain personal data (ticket personalization). This measure is used when events are particularly high-risk. The organizer is allowed to keep the collected personal data for a maximum of three months after the event. After that, he must destroy it.

98. M. Nunič, *Zakon o javnih zbiranjih s komentarjem*, 79 (GV Založba 2011).
99. M. Nunič, *Zakon o javnih zbiranjih s komentarjem*, 54 (GV Založba 2011).
100. Official Journal of SFRY, No. 14/1990.
101. Official Journal of Slovenia, Nos 70/03 and 96/05.

129. In a separate chapter, the law prescribes the conditions for organizing road sports events (cycling, moto-sport). In such cases the deadlines are a bit longer whereas this is usually the responsibility of several authorities. The organizer must also obtain a roadblock permit.

III. Sports Specifics in the Restrictions on the Use of Alcohol Act

130. Restrictions on the Use of Alcohol Act[102] contain some provisions regarding sports events. These measures are also based on the European Convention on Spectator Violence and Misbehavior at Sports Events and in particular at Football Matches.

131. The Act generally forbids the sale or supply of alcohol in facilities and on the adjoining lands where any public event according to the Public Assembly Act is organized. This ban is valid for the duration of the event. The organizer is allowed to sell alcohol only if he obtains special permission.

132. Certain special provisions apply to sporting events. The first is that one hour before the start, and during a public sporting event, the sale or supply of alcoholic beverages containing more than 15% by volume of alcohol is prohibited in sports facilities and associated land.

133. The second is that the sale or supply of alcoholic beverages on sporting events is allowed only in open disposable paper, plastic and tin containers.

134. In the case of a public sporting event for which, in accordance with the regulations governing public gatherings, the necessary permission of the competent authority is needed, in the sports facility and on the associated lands, the organizer must determine and visibly mark the premises and areas where the sale or supply and consumption of alcoholic beverages is allowed. The organizer must also ensure control of the intake of alcoholic beverages on premises and areas where consumption is prohibited.

135. Additionally, at least one of the following warnings must be prominently displayed on the premises or surfaces the referred to in the preceding paragraph: 'The Minister of Health warns: Drinking alcohol can be detrimental to health!' Or 'The Minister of Health warns: Drinking excessive alcohol is detrimental to health!'.

136. Despite having a licence, the organizer may decide by himself not to sell or offer alcoholic beverages one hour before the start and during the public sporting event in order to protect order, public order, security of property or people. He will adopt such measure in case of a medium or high-risk public sport event. In the case

102. Official Journal of Slovenia, Nos 15/03 and 27/17.

of a high-risk public sport event for which the organizer is required to obtain a permit, the competent authority may, to increase the safety of persons and property and to maintain order, prohibit the organizer to sell or supply of alcoholic beverages.

IV. Organizer's Tort Liability

137. According to Article 157 of the Code of Obligations, the organizer of the gathering of a large number of people indoors or outdoors is liable for damage caused by death or personal injury resulting from extraordinary circumstances that may occur on such occasions (e.g., crowd movements, general disorder and the like).

138. At public events where there are crowds, the risk of harm is increased.[103] Because a crowd is legally a dangerous thing, the damage that occurs in the event of an emergency is objectively the responsibility of the event organizer.[104] In such cases, it is often impossible to find the one who caused the damage,[105] so it is justified that the organizer who caused such increased risk is liable for damages that result from it.

§7. Tax

I. General Issues

139. Article 5 of the Sports Act states that Slovenia pursues public interest in the sport with a simulative fiscal policy. This is a programme norm and is not directly enforceable, but it is still a commitment of the state to help the sport with tax incentives. Below I will briefly show how this programme norm is realized in valid tax legislation on taxation of sport clubs and sport federations. Taxation of athletes is discussed in Part II.

140. According to Article 50 of Financial Administration Act,[106] these subjects have to be registered in tax register:

– legal entities that are registered in a court register;
– individuals (natural persons) permanently residing in Slovenia;
– individuals (natural persons) temporarily residing in Slovenia;
– sole entrepreneurs;

103. S. Cigoj, *Komentar obligacijskih razmerij*, 707 (Časopisni zavod Uradni list SR Slovenije 1984).
104. S. Perović & D. Stojanović (eds), *Komentar Zakona o obligacionim odnosima*, Book I, 540 (Pravni fakultet Kragujevac 1980).
105. M. Juhart & N. Plavšak (eds), *Obligacijski zakonik s komentarjem*, Book I, 904 (GV Založba 2003).
106. Official Journal of the Republic of Slovenia, No. 25/14.

- legal entities and individuals (natural persons) engaged in the business that are registered in a non-court register;[107]
- natural and legal persons who do not have their headquarters or are not otherwise registered in Slovenia, but are operating on its territory;
- associations of persons under foreign law that are without legal personality;
- direct users of state or municipal budget;[108] and
- persons not covered by the previous points.

141. According to the content of Article 50 of the Financial Administration Act, all legal forms that are permanently practising sports in Slovenia have to be registered for tax purposes. Of course, if an athlete or a sport club comes to Slovenia to participate in a sporting event this is not considered as permanent sport practice on Slovenian territory, and no tax registration is needed. However, this does not mean that no tax liabilities arise of such a participation if athlete or sport club is entitled to or receive payment for their participation on the territory. Since this tax analysis would go far beyond the purpose of this monograph, I will not describe it. I will therefore just make a short description of tax liabilities that arise for sport clubs, sport federations and companies that compete, if they have a Slovenian tax residence (they have a tax status in Slovenia). I will briefly describe a general tax legislation;[109] tax incentives connected to sports are presented in a more detailed manner.

II. Tax Status of Sport Societies

A. *Corporate Income Tax Act*

142. According to the Corporate Income Tax Act,[110] taxpayers are legal entities of domestic and foreign law and associations without legal personality that are not taxable persons according to Personal Income Tax Act.[111] Slovenian tax residents are liable to pay tax on all worldwide income (worldwide taxation); non-residents are only liable to pay tax on income that is originating in Slovenia (source taxation). Subject to taxation is resident's or a non-resident's profit, earned by the activity and/or business performed by him/her either in or through a business unit in Slovenia and resident's or a non-resident's income, subject to withholding tax under Corporate Income Tax Act. The tax base of a resident and non-resident in respect of

107. For example, registers of professional sportsmen and private workers in sport for which Ministry of Education, Science and Sport is competent.
108. For example, ministries.
109. More about taxation in Slovenia in 2018 at: http://www.mf.gov.si/fileadmin/mf.gov.si/pageuploads/Davki_in_carine/Angle%C5%A1ki/Taxation_in_Slovenia_2018.pdf (accessed 9 Aug. 2019).
110. Official Journal of Slovenia, Nos 117/06, 56/08, 76/08, 5/09, 96/09, 110/09 – ZDavP-2B, 43/10, 59/11, 24/12, 30/12, 94/12, 81/13, 50/14, 23/15, 82/15, 68/16, 69/17 and 79/18.
111. Official Journal of Slovenia, Nos 13/11 (Official Consolidated Text), 9/12, 24/12, 30/12, 40/12, 75/12, 94/12, 52/13, 96/13, 29/14, 50/14, 23/15, 55/15, 63/16, 69/17, 21/19 and 28/19.

activities and/or business performed either in or through a business unit in Slovenia is the profit (the surplus of revenue over expenses). The tax base for withholding tax is each individual gross income.

143. In general, any income is revenue, but non-profit taxpayers are entitled to a special tax treatment. Sport associations can use a tax exemption if they have a legal form of sport society or federation under the Societies Act and are actually operating according to the purpose of their establishment and operation. These associations are not fully exempted from taxation; they just do not pay tax on so-called non-profit activity (non-profit income), but still pay tax on their profit activity (profit income). The Financial Minister has the authority to define profit and non-profit activity taking into account that profit activity is performed in the market to gain profit, that through performing profit activity the taxpayer competes in the market with other persons and other types of the legal entity of taxpayer.

144. The Ministry of Finance adopted rules concerning definitions of profitable and non-profitable activity.[112] According to these rules examples of non-profit income, typical for sport clubs are donations,[113] membership and subscription fees, bequests and inheritances, public purpose funds. Profit income, typical for sport clubs, are in particular income from sales of goods and services, rents and other payments, income realized on the disposal of fixed assets, gaming income, broadcasting rights income, income from transfer of players and tickets income.[114]

145. As was already mentioned, non-profit taxpayers are exempted from paying tax on income from non-profit activities (income), but since tax recognizable are only those expenses that are required to acquire taxable income, some expenses have to be eliminated from tax base calculation. Because it is often hard to make a split between these two types of expenses,[115] Corporate Income Tax Act allows that non-profit taxpayers determine the tax base using a proportion of all costs and they do not need calculate the actual cost as is a rule for all other taxpayers.

B. Value Added Tax Act

146. Value Added Tax (VAT) is a turnover tax.[116] It taxes transactions, namely:

112. Official Journal of Slovenia, Nos 109/07 and 68/09.
113. I emphasize that donors that are either legal persons or natural persons who are practising business can use tax deductions for donations to (among others) sport clubs and federations. The maximum tax deduction is 0.3% of their taxable income. Personal income taxpayers can additionally give each year a maximum of 0.5% of tax to (among others) sport clubs or federations that act in the public interest instead to public budget.
114. More about income from profit and non-profit activity, *see* J. Podlipnik, *Pravni in davčni status športnih klubov*, 147–190 (PhD Thesis, Law faculty in Ljubljana 2010).
115. For example, a rented clubhouse is used for profit and non-profit activities.
116. B. Terra & J. Kajus, *Introduction to European VAT*, 271 (IBFD 2011).

- supplies of goods for consideration within the territory of the Republic of Slovenia by taxable persons in the course of their economic activities;
- certain intra-Community acquisitions of goods for consideration within the territory of Slovenia;
- supplies of services for consideration within the territory of Slovenia by taxable persons in the course of their economic activities; and
- importations of goods.

147. Taxable person is anyone who independently, carries out in any place any economic activity, whatever be the purpose or results of that activity. Economic activity shall comprise any production, manufacturing, trading and service activity, including mining, agricultural and professional activity. The exploitation of tangible and intangible property for the purpose of obtaining income therefrom on a continuing basis shall also be regarded as an economic activity.

148. This means that sport clubs and federations can be taxable persons for VAT purposes as long as they carry out economic activities. Not all taxable persons have the obligation to charge VAT on their taxable transactions, but only if they are either voluntarily identified or they have an obligation to identify for VAT. Compulsory identification generally arises when taxable persons turnover within a period of twelve months exceed EUR 50,000. Especially for bigger sport clubs and federations public funding will not be sufficient, and they will have to carry out economic activities in order to 'survive' in the long run.

149. There are two VAT exemptions that are used by sport clubs and federations. The first one is an exemption for the supply of services closely linked to sport or physical education by non-profit-making organizations to persons[117] taking part in sport or physical education. The second exemption does not mention the word 'sport' but allows that supplies of goods and services by non-profit sport organizations are exempt from VAT if these supplies are in connection with fund-raising events organized by these organizations on an occasional basis and exclusively for their own benefit, provided that such exemption is not likely to cause distortion of market competition.[118]

C. *Inheritance and Gift Taxation Act*[119]

150. Associations that are established to perform sporting activities are not exempted from taxation as is the case for some other activities that are in the public

117. Court of Justice of the European Union in Case C-253/07 interpreted that the term 'person' includes services supplied to corporate persons and to unincorporated associations and not only to natural persons.
118. More about these two exemptions, *see* J. Podlipnik, *Pravni in davčni status športnih klubov*, 229–233 (PhD Thesis, Law faculty in Ljubljana 2010).
119. Official Journal of Slovenia, Nos 117/06 and 36/16.

interest.[120] This means that inheritances and gifts (donations) received from one person by sport clubs or sport federations are taxed under this act if they exceed EUR 5,000[121] in twelve-month period.[122]

III. Sport Federations

151. Sport federations are special forms of sport associations (societies), and hence everything that is written in the previous chapter about them, also applies to sport federations.

IV. Associated Companies Which Enforce Competition Licence

152. I have mentioned above that some sport federations allow that sport societies establish a legal entity in the legal form of a company which then competes. Such company is a taxpayer (taxable person) according to Corporate Income Tax Act and if it is performing taxable transactions also a taxpayer (taxable person) according to Value Added Tax Act. These companies are generally not entitled to tax incentives that apply to non-profit associations and were mentioned above, since these companies are not non-profit organizations. An exception to this rule could be VAT exemption for sporting service, since Value Added Tax Act states that this exemption can be used even if sporting service is not provided by a non-profit organization if such service provider priory notifies tax authority in electronic form and if one or more of the following conditions are fulfilled:

- sporting services by such taxable person are not provided to make a profit, but if a profit is made it must not be distributed, but has to be assigned to the continuance or improvement of the services supplied;
- these taxpayers must be managed and administered on an essentially voluntary basis by persons who have no direct or indirect interest, either themselves or through intermediaries, in the results of the activities concerned;
- taxpayers charge prices which are approved by the competent authorities or which do not exceed such approved prices or, in respect of those services not subject to approval, prices lower than those charged for similar services by taxable persons subject to VAT;
- this exemption for the services concerned is not likely to cause distortion of competition on the market to the disadvantage of taxable persons subject to VAT.

---

120. Religious, philanthropic, charitable, health, social care, education, research and cultural activities, protection and rescue activities.
121. If an inheritance or a gift is given in the form of a real estate, it is taxed regardless of its value.
122. More about inheritance and gift taxation of sport associations, *see* J. Podlipnik, *Zakon o davku na dediščine in darila*, 33–35 and 69–71 (GV Založba 2013).

153. Received inheritances and gifts (donations) are not taxed under the Inheritance and Gift Taxation Act, but they are income under the Corporate Income Tax Act, since non-profit exemption in latter act is not applicable to companies.

§8. SPORTS JUSTICE

I. General Issues

154. Disputes in sports can theoretically be resolved in the same way as other types of disputes. However, the specific nature of the sport (e.g., short career duration) often requires a very efficient procedure. Courts are not best suited for this task due to rigid rules, lengthy proceedings and lack of knowledge of sports law.[123] Nevertheless, the courts also decide on sports-related disputes, as is also confirmed by publicly available case law. [124] While of course all alternatives to dispute resolution (e.g., arbitration, mediation, conciliation) are also possible,[125] most sports disputes are resolved through arbitration.

155. The reason is the pyramid structure of European sport. In fact, if athletes wish to pursue a career in certain sport, they have no choice but to agree with the rules of the sports organization, thereby indirectly agreeing to the national and international jurisdiction of the arbitral tribunal and the rules of procedure by which it operates.

156. I will not deal with CAS in this monograph, because it is only indirectly related to Slovenia. After the presentation of the Arbitration Act,[126] I will also briefly show the autonomous arrangement according to the rules of the Slovenian Football Association and the Slovenian Ski Association.

II. Arbitration Act

157. Arbitration is one way of out-of-court dispute resolution, as the dispute is not settled before state judicial authorities.[127] The arbitration is composed of one or more persons agreed upon by the parties and entrusted, by mutual agreement and voluntarily, with the issuance of a decision of merit, which is equated by law with the final judgment of a (regular) court. By concluding an arbitration agreement, the

123. M. Gornik, *Razreševanje sporov v športu*, 357 (V. Bergant Rakočević ed., *Šport & pravo*, GV Založba 2008).
124. For example, conclusion of the Supreme Court, I Up 490/2009 (7. Sep. 2010), where the question was which court has jurisdiction to rule on the legality of an athlete transferring from one club to another.
125. M. Gornik, *Razreševanje sporov v športu*, 361–362 (V. Bergant Rakočević ed., *Šport & pravo*, GV Založba 2008).
126. Official Journal of Slovenia, No. 45/08.
127. L. Ude et al., *Zakon o arbitraži s pojasnili*, 153 (GV Založba 2010).

parties exclude the jurisdiction of (ordinary) courts.[128] Arbitration, unlike other alternative dispute resolution methods, is most similar to litigation.

158. Arbitration Act applies to arbitrations domiciled in the Republic of Slovenia, regardless of whether the parties to the proceedings are domestic or foreign. Any property claim may be the subject of an arbitration agreement. Other claims may be subject to an arbitration agreement only if the parties can settle the claim. An arbitration agreement is an agreement of the parties to submit to the arbitration any or all disputes which have already arisen or which may arise in connection with a particular contractual or non-contractual legal relationship. The arbitration agreement may take the form of an arbitration clause in the contract or in the form of an independent agreement. The arbitration agreement must be concluded in writing. The agreement is concluded in writing if it is contained in a document signed by the parties and if it is concluded by the exchange of letters, faxes, telegrams, e-mail or other means of communication or storage of data that provide an accessible and subsequently suitable record of the arbitration agreement. If the contract refers to another document containing an arbitration clause, the arbitration agreement is valid, if the arbitration clause is an integral part of the contract.

159. The parties determine the number of arbitrators. If the parties do not determine the number of arbitrators, there are three arbitrators. The parties to the arbitration proceedings are equal. Each party must be guaranteed the right to be heard. An arbitration decision has the effect of a final judgment between the parties. The parties may challenge the arbitrational decision before a court only by an action for its annulment. The parties may not waive this right in advance. An action for the annulment of an arbitrational decision must be filed within three months of the day on which the party filing the complaint received it. The grounds for challenging the decision are very limited. They relate to the validity of the arbitration agreement, its content, the constitution of the arbitration panel, some of the most serious violations of procedure and violations of public policy.[129] Arbitrational decisions are not yet enforceable, but special judicial proceedings must be conducted to this end. The scope of the court's judgment depends on whether it is domestic or foreign arbitrational decision.

III. Slovenian Football Association

160. The executive board of the Slovenian Football Association has adopted comprehensive rules on Arbitration.[130] The arbitration is a one-stage and procedure. The Football Association has a permanent arbitration body. Its jurisdiction is to decide on:

---

128. L. Ude, *Arbitražno pravo*, 23 (GV Založba 2004).

129. L. Ude et al., *Zakon o arbitraži s pojasnili*, 178 (GV Založba 2010).

130. Available only in Slovenian language at: https://www.nzs.si/Doc/Pravilnik%20o%20Arbitra%C5%BEi_V2.0._19062019.pdf (accessed 9 Aug. 2019).

- disputes arising from the contractual relationship between football clubs, players, coaches and agents;
- compensation disputes for unjustified withdrawal of the contract and compensation for the education and training of the player between football clubs;
- other disputes arising out of contractual relations in the field of football, if so agreed in the arbitration agreement; and
- disputes concerning the application of regulations, instructions and decisions of the football association, and other disputes arising from sports-competition relations, if so prescribed.

161. The arbitration tribunal renders its decisions using applicable laws, provisions of the statute, regulations and other regulations of the Slovenian Football Association. If the rules of the Slovenian Football Association do not comply with the regulations of the UEFA and FIFA, the provisions of the regulations of these two organizations apply *mutatis mutandis.*

162. Slovenian Football Association, its members, their members, leagues, club associations, officials, players, their agents and FIFA and UEFA match agents are obliged to resolve the above-mentioned disputes before arbitration and respect its decisions.

163. In addition to what was described, the Rules on Arbitration precisely regulate the organization of the arbitration, the basic provisions of the arbitration procedure, the course of the arbitration procedure and the arbitration decision. A more detailed account of these rules would go beyond the purpose of this monograph. It is interesting to note that the provisions of the Contentious Civil Procedure Act[131] apply *mutatis mutandis* to issues not directly governed by the Rules.

IV. Slovenian Ski Association

164. The provisions of Rules of Procedure of the Honorary Tribunal[132] are extremely short. It just deals with the number of arbiters (three) which are elected by the General Assembly. The members of the Honorary Tribunal elect its president between themselves. The Honorary Tribunal can render decision if at least two members are present (quorum). A decision is validly taken if it is voted in by a majority of all members. A member of the Tribunal must be excluded if there is a conflict of interest. The work of the court is not public, but the Tribunal may decide otherwise.

131. Official Journal of Slovenia, Nos 73/07 (Official Consolidated Text), 45/08, 45/08, 111/08, 57/09, 12/10, 50/10, 107/10, 75/12, 40/13, 92/13, 10/14, 48/15, 6/17, 10/17 and 16/19.

132. Available only in Slovenian language at: https://www.sloski.si/resources/files/pdf/Pravilnik_o_delu_astnega_razsodia.pdf (accessed 9 Aug. 2019).

Part II. Sport and Employment

Chapter 1. General Issues

165. In this part of the monograph, we go beyond the mere description of employment relationship between players and clubs. We also deal with special status of athletes in general under Sports Act and under the rules of sport federations.

166. We have mostly dealt with the organization of sport on a national level and have shown that clubs play an important role in the pyramid structure. In order to demonstrate the whole picture, we must not forget about national teams. In this case, there is a direct legal relationship between athletes (members of national teams) and sport federations or OCS (national team). In most sports, national team competitions are rare; athletes have their club careers (football, etc.). However, in other sports (skiing, etc.) important competitions happen on national team level. To be able to compete in those competitions that are also financially lucrative, athletes must be members of national teams. In state competitions (national level), these athletes still compete for their clubs, but at international level they compete for their country as members of the national team.

167. Freedom of work according to Article 49 of the Constitution prescribes three different elements: freedom of employment, prohibition of forced labour and the right to access of employment under equal position. It must be noted that this article does not guarantee work as it is often wrongly interpreted.

168. We usually do not consider athletes as workers, since practising sports for a living has many peculiarities that make this kind of work special in comparison with 'regular' work (working hours, working period), but in some cases, especially in collective sports (football, etc.), where athletes are part of the team, they could be considered as workers. Later, we will see what conditions Slovenian Employment Relationships Act[133] prescribes for someone to be considered as a worker. In this case, this article of Constitution protects him.

169. Freedom of work is also connected with two other constitutional provisions which will not be expressly dealt with in this monograph, as they are not directly connected to sport and status: Freedom of Trade Unions (Article 76) and Right to Strike (Article 77).

133. Official Journal of the Republic of Slovenia, No. 21/13.

170. Article 76 of the Constitution guarantees the freedom to establish, operate and join trade unions. This provision is not limited to persons who have a status of an employee (worker). A good example for this is a Slovenian Athletes Union, whose members may become all athletes who are or have been registered in the sport clubs in the Republic of Slovenia and the athletes who are citizens of Slovenia, registered in sport clubs outside the Republic of Slovenia (Article 1 of Statute).[134]

171. Article 77 states: 'Employees have the right to strike. Where required by the public interest, the right to strike may be restricted by law, with due consideration given to the type and nature of activity involved.' In comparison to Article 76, the right to strike is expressly reserved to employees, but a person can be an employee (a worker) in the sense of Article 77 even if he did not conclude a contract of employment, if elements of the legal employment relationship are met. That is the reason why Slovenian football players have already been striking (e.g., in 2008),[135] although almost all of them have concluded civil law (and not employment) contracts with their clubs.

134. Statute is available in English language at: http://www.sportnik.si/design/uploads/content//STATUT%20SsS_ANGL.pdf (accessed 29 Jul. 2020).

135. *See* http://www.24ur.com/sport/nogomet/jutri-stavka-slovenskih-nogometasev.html (accessed 29 Jul. 2020).

Chapter 2. Sources of Employment Law (Ordinary Law and CBA)

§1. Legal Status of Athletes

I. Sports Act

A. *Status of an Athlete*

172. According to Sports Act, an athlete is an individual who is properly registered in the register of registered and categorized athletes. An individual can register as an athlete if he:

– is at least 12 years old;
– is a member of a sport association that is a member of national sport federation; and
– has confirmed his participation in the competition of the official competition system by OCS.

173. An athlete is also an individual under 12 years of age, but not under 10 years of age, who is registered in the Olympic sports disciplines of individual sports, in which athletes under 18 may participate in world championships in the adult category.

B. *Status of a Categorized Athlete*

174. A categorized athlete is an athlete who is:

– a citizen of the Republic of Slovenia;
– at least 14 years old; and
– has the status of youth, national, promising, international, world or Olympic class. Athletes are assigned to these classes according to the results they have achieved in competitions that are a part of an official competition system. The official competition system is a system of competitions in the Republic of Slovenia and international competitions in individual sports, which is classified according to their mutual competitiveness, is in accordance with the rules of national sport federations or the rules of international sport federations and approved by OCS. The competent expert council of the OCS specifies the conditions and criteria for the registration and categorization of athletes, separately for individual and separately for collective sports and publishes them on the website of the competent ministry and the OCS.

C. Status of a Professional Athlete

175. According to the Sports Act, a professional athlete is any athlete, who registered in a special professional athletes register under this Act, independently performs work in sport as his/her exclusive or supplementary activity and is at least 15 years old. An application to register as a professional sportsman must be filed with the Ministry of Education, Science and Sport. Whether an athlete is engaged in sports for a living (professional who earns enough money) or not and whether his sport discipline is individual or collective plays no role.

D. Status of a Top Athlete

176. A top athlete is a categorized athlete of international, world or Olympic class who has achieved a top result in an international competition in the adult category and is entered in the register of registered and categorized athletes as a top athlete.

E. Rights and Obligations of Athletes According to Their Status

177. The Sports Act also prescribes certain rights and obligations that concern athletes in general and those that apply to individual categories of athletes. This is actually the main purpose of different athlete statuses.

1. Right to Transfer to Another Sport Organization

178. Article 34 of Sports Act allows athletes to transfer from a sport organization to another sports organization[136] (e.g., a sport club). A sport organization may demand payment of a transfer compensation from an athlete over the age of 15 if it has concluded a written contract with it stipulating this and according to which it receives a payment at least gross minimum wage in the Republic of Slovenia.[137] However, a sport organization may not demand payment of compensation if the actual costs covered by the athlete for preparation and competitions in official competition systems are higher than the payment referred to in the preceding paragraph.

136. According to Sports Act, a sport organization is an entity with a legal personality and with one of the following statutes:

- sport associations and sport federations registered in the Republic of Slovenia;
- sport associations and sport associations of Slovenes abroad in Italy, Austria and Hungary;
- sport institutes under this Act;
- legal entities registered to perform activities in sports in the Republic of Slovenia; and
- institutions established for a generally useful purpose in the field of sport, in accordance with the law governing the institutions.

137. In 2020 it amounts to EUR 940.58.

This actually means that a sport organization can claim reimbursement for the costs it has incurred with the athlete's development.

2. Rights of Individuals with a Status of an Athlete

179. An individual who has a status of an athlete according to Sports Act has:

- Rights related to education:
  - the right to the adjustment of school and study obligations to the extent and in the manner determined by the regulations governing the field of education or the field of higher education;
  - the right to enrol in further education under more favourable conditions; and
  - the right to take the high-school graduation diploma exam (abitur) in two consecutive terms, in case of an athlete who participated in a major international competition under the Sports Act in the year of the exam; in this case, it is considered that they have passed the exam in the first term.
- Health-related rights:
  - a right to a safe process of sports training;
  - a right to preventive healthcare in accordance with the regulations governing healthcare and health insurance; and
  - the right not to train or compete during illness or injury.

180. Athletes who received the Bloudek Lifetime Achievement Award also have the right to an exceptional pension. We will discuss this exceptional pension latter on.[138]

3. Rights of Top Athletes

181. In addition to the rights that all registered athletes have, top athletes also have the right to employment in the public sector. We will discuss this later on.[139]

182. In addition to other rights of registered athletes, top athletes, who are winners of an Olympic or a medal from the World Championships in Olympic collective sports or Olympic sports disciplines of individual sports, have the right to:

- the reimbursement of the costs of education for the acquisition of education according to publicly valid educational programmes in the Republic of Slovenia, once at each level of education that has not yet been acquired, or qualification for professional work in sports under Sports Act; and
- an exceptional pension.[140]

138. *See* §6. Social Security.
139. *See* §2. Employment Relationship.
140. *See* §6. Social Security.

4. Obligations of Athletes Who Have a Status of a National Team Member

183. An athlete who competes in the competition of the official competition system for the national team of the Republic of Slovenia has to wear sportswear in green, blue or white, which has the coat of arms or flag of the Republic of Slovenia. He has this obligation unless it is contrary to the competition rules of international sport federations or rules of the IOC.

II. Sport Federations

A. General Issues

184. Athletes who wish to compete in competitions organized by sport federations have to be registered. With this registration, they acquire a status and undertake to observe the rules that the sport federation has enacted. These rules sometimes also govern issues related to the issues addressed in this part of the monograph (e.g., the content of contracts between athletes and sport clubs). This is the rule for so-called collective sport disciplines (football, basketball, ice hockey, etc.), but in individual sport disciplines (skiing, tennis, etc.) athletes usually choose to compete for clubs, but they can also compete even if they are not members of the clubs. In the latter case, sport federations regularly still demand registration of these 'freelance' athletes. Even if they are allowed to participate (usually not on a regular basis, but only in some competitions) they must comply with the competition rules, set by the organizer of the competition, which is usually a sport federation itself or a direct or indirect member of such sport federation. This means that indirectly such 'freelancers' are formally not part of the pyramid structure of sport, but still have to follow most of the rules (e.g., doping rules) set by sport federation that allows 'freelancers' to compete.

B. Football Association of Slovenia

185. Football players are only allowed to participate in competitions organized by Slovenian Football Association if they are registered according to Regulation on the Registration and status of players (Article 6).[141] With registration, football players undertake to respect the rules of Slovenian Football Association, UEFA and FIFA. A player may only be registered for one club at a time and for a maximum of three clubs within the same competition season and during this period may play in official matches for a maximum of two clubs. There are also other restrictions regarding the deadlines in which transfers of player between clubs can be made, etc.

186. Football players are registered as either amateurs or professionals. A football player is a professional if he concludes a written contract with his club and

141. Available only in Slovenian language at: https://www.nzs.si/Doc/PRSI%20V5.0_19062019_%C4%8Distopis_final.pdf (accessed 30 Jul. 2020).

receives from his club for playing football remuneration that exceeds his actual costs incurred by playing football. The lowest average monthly payment of professional player to play football must not be lower than the minimum wage in the Republic of Slovenia.[142] All other players are considered amateurs for the purpose of this national federation.

187. For this monograph, it is crucial that the registration procedure is carried out by Slovenian Football Association. Applications for registrations are filed by clubs, but football players must give their consent for the registration. Written contract must be attached to the application if the club wishes to register a professional player. If a professional player is foreigner (players from other EU Member States are not considered as such), then working permit or proof that application to obtain one was filed, must be attached to the application to register.

188. Since no player can be registered for two clubs at the same time, an athlete's written statement must be attached that he has not yet been registered. If he is already registered for another club, this club must give the new club a declaration that he has no objections for this player to register for another club. If a player was registered for a club from abroad, the player can be registered for Slovenian club only if a club receives an international transfer certificate from abroad.

C. Ski Association of Slovenia

189. According to the Regulations regarding registration of competitors,[143] skiers must be registered to be allowed to participate in competitions organized by Slovenian Ski Association. The same applies to competitions organized by FIS and IBU. Since competitors are primarily not clubs, but athletes themselves, as skiing is an individual sport, skiers have the right to compete in all competitions even if they are not members of ski clubs, but they have to be direct members of Slovenian Ski Association.[144] Exceptions are made for foreigners, who do not receive championship points.[145]

---

142. Currently at least EUR 940.58.
143. Available only in Slovenian language at: http://www.sloski.si/resources/files/pdf/Registracijski%20pravilnik09.pdf (accessed 30 Jul. 2020).
144. These are so-called extraordinary members. We believe that this membership is contrary to the Societies Act, since members of associations of societies can only be societies. Besides that articles of association forbids extraordinary members to participate in competition system, but other acts of Slovenian Ski Association allow extraordinary members to compete. Rules are therefore mutually inconsistent and inconsistent with the practice.
145. Competition system in alpine skiing is available only in Slovenian language at: http://www.sloski.si/resources/files/pdf/alpsko-smucanje/12-13/Tekmovalni-sistem-v-alpskem-smucanju-2013.pdf (accessed 30 Jul. 2020).

§2. Employment Relationship

I. General Issues

190. The Sports Act also deals in part with labour (employment) law issues. According to general rule in Article 59, the employment relations of athletes are subject to the law governing employment relations, i.e., Employment Relationships Act. However, immediately afterwards, the Sports Act provides for exceptions to this rule, which is logical, since the work of athletes is specific compared to 'normal' employees. In the case of concluding an employment contract with an athlete, the contracting parties may, in the employment contract, regardless of the restrictions set by the Employment Relationships Act, regulate the rights, obligations and responsibilities arising from the employment relationship in relation to:

- the conditions and restrictions of a fixed-term employment relationship;[146]
- working hours;
- providing breaks and rests;
- payment for work;
- disciplinary responsibility;
- termination of the employment contract; and
- an obligation to publicly announce a job vacancy.

Sports Act does not have a provision that would exclude the rule from Article 13 of the Employment Relationships Act, according to which work may not be performed on the basis of civil law contracts, except in cases determined by law. This means that clubs and athletes are generally obligated to conclude employment contract if elements of employment relationship exist.[147] These elements are defined by the following definition of an employment relationship (Article 4 of the Employment Relationships Act): 'An employment relationship is a relationship between an employee and an employer in which the employee voluntarily joins the employer's organized work process and performs paid work in person and continuously and under the supervision of the employer.' The practice in Slovenian sports shows that sport clubs conclude employment contracts with athletes only exceptionally. Civil law contracts are usually concluded between them. The reasons for this are mainly of a tax nature, as athletes pay less taxes and social security contributions if they receive payment as self-employed persons (e.g., as professional athletes or sole proprietors). The competent authorities tolerate such a practice, as it has not been publicly perceived that the labour and tax inspectorate would address this problem.

146. Irrespective of the provisions of the law governing employment relations on the restriction of concluding fixed-term employment contracts for the performance of the same work, an athlete may conclude several successive fixed-term employment contracts with the same employer. The continuous duration of these contracts may not exceed ten years. A break of three months or less does not mean an interruption of the uninterrupted ten-year period referred to in the previous sentence.

147. Cf. R. Brajnik et al., *Problematika delovnopravnega položaja športnih trenerjev s poudarkom na nogometu*, 24.

Athletes, however, generally have no interest in requesting the establishment of an employment relationship, although they could do so if elements exist.[148]

II. Self-Employment

191. Most athletes in Slovenia are not workers, but are self-employed. However, since, as a rule, self-employed athletes obtain income from one person (i.e., sport club), they are in fact either 'hidden' workers or at least economically dependent persons.[149]

192. As self-employed, athletes must acquire a special status. This is either the status of a professional athlete under the Sports Act or the status of a sole proprietor under the Companies Act.[150] There are no significant practical differences between the two statuses from the point of view of the business itself.

III. Employment of Top Athletes in Public Administration

A. General Issues

193. Since independence, Slovenia has supported top sports with employment of top athletes and top coaches in public administration. Prior to the enactment of the current Sports Act, these issues were regulated by a contract between some ministries (Ministry of Defence – Slovenian Army; Ministry of the Internal Affairs – Police; and the Ministry of Finance – Financial administration) and the OCS. This has been problematic from the point of view of the principle of legality. Today, these issues are regulated in Articles 63–65 of the Sports Act. There are two reasons why Slovenia is supporting top sport in this way: to promote Slovenia internationally and to support and help top athletes (Article 63 of Sports Act). Since Slovenia is a small country and its public interest as sport is supposed to be for the public good because of the positive effect that it has on the society, and as by top sporting results, Slovenia is promoting itself. Because of its size, Slovenia must seize every opportunity for promotion that has positive effects on other industries, e.g., tourism. Due to Slovenia's size, athletes have less opportunity to obtain sufficient funds in the market, e.g., by exploiting their personal rights, which is generally the case for less commercially interesting sports.

194. Through employment in the public sector, top athletes become civil servants and are subject to these rules. Nevertheless, their employment relationships

148. G. Strban & L. Mišič, *Socialne pravice športnikov in trenerjev*, 190 (V. Bergant Rakočević ed., *Šport in pravo*, Inštitut za lokalno samoupravo in javna naročila 2020).

149. *Ibid.*, 191.

150. Official Journal of the Republic of Slovenia, Nos 65/09 (Official Consolidated Text), 33/11, 91/11, 32/12, 57/12, 44/13, 82/13, 55/15, 15/17 and 22/19.

are specific, so the Sports Act explicitly stipulates that the specifics of concluding an employment contract prescribed by this act also apply.[151]

195. The recruitment of top athletes is carried out by first creating a priority list of athletes to be recruited. The priority list is formed according to the following criteria (criteria): achieved result in a major international competition or fulfilled norm for participation in a major international competition. The law leaves a more detailed definition of the criteria to the OCS. As the number of athletes employed in public administration is limited, the athletes actually employed by the state are then selected from this priority list. Currently, three ministries or their organizational units employ athletes: the Ministry of Defence (Slovenian Army), the Ministry of the Internal Affairs (Police) and the Ministry of Finance (Financial Administration).

B. *Special Rights and Obligations of Employed Top Athletes*

196. Top athletes can be employed with the Ministries until they retain their top athlete status. They receive a salary, have the right to annual leave and all other rights that ordinary employees have. But they are not ordinary employees since they do not come to work to the office every day, their main job is to train to compete. To achieve the best results they can, they have special obligations and rights. Their rights and obligations are individually agreed in each employment contract, but the agreement specifies what employment contracts must include.

197. Special obligations of employed top athletes:

- to compete in international army, police and financial administration competitions as members of these public bodies, if this does not intervene with their regular competitions;
- to participate in the promotional, protocol and other events organized by the Ministries;
- to assist with their knowledge in training of other workers of these ministries by demonstrating sport, preparing sports programmes and analysing work;
- to attend the prescribed training for their job;
- to maintain in top physical form for achieving top sports results; and
- to regularly submit reports about their work and achievements to the employer.

198. Special rights of employed top athletes are:

- financing or provision of adequate equipment needed for competitions in which they represent their employers;
- to train without disturbance by the employer;
- to participate in coordination with the calendar of general sporting competitions and with competitions for the employer;
- to compete for their sport clubs and sport federations; and

151. *See* general issues above.

– to be educated in order to attain sports or employer's qualifications.

C. Sports in Which Top Athletes Are Currently Employed

199. List of athletes who are employed by the Ministries is published on the internet.[152] Athletes that are employed by the ministries practise different sports, such as: athletics (track), biathlon, gymnastics, judo, cycling (road and mountain bike), archery, motocross, speedway, table tennis, paragliding, parachuting, swimming, wrestling, skiing (alpine, cross-country, freestyle, biathlon, snowboarding, Nordic combination, ski jumping), shooting, climbing (indoor and alpine), taekwondo, triathlon, rowing, kayaking, canoeing, sailing and ju-jitsu. The vast majority are individual sport disciplines (e.g., there are no football, basketball, handball or hockey players).

IV. Collective Bargaining Agreement

200. Although some have been striving for this for several years, there is no collective agreement in Slovenia that would regulate the rights and obligations of athletes. Athletes who are civil servants are subject to a collective agreement for the public sector, but this does not regulate the specifics of sport.

§3. Fundamental Rights and Obligations of Associations and Athletes

I. Public Regulation

201. As already mentioned, associations (e.g., clubs) and athletes are also required to enter into an employment contract when the elements of the employment relationship set out in the Employment Relationships Act are met. In this case, the association and the athlete have all the rights and obligations prescribed by labour law. These are not only the rights and obligations set out in the Employment Relationships Act, but also those prescribed by other labour law legislations (e.g., the obligation to pay the minimum wage). According to the Employment Relationships Act, an employed athlete must thus perform the work, follow the instructions of the club, refrain from causing harm, protect business secrets, abandon the performance of the same work for the competition, etc. The association is obliged to provide work and payment for it, to protect the privacy of the employed athlete and to ensure safe working conditions, to pay severance pay, etc.

202. However, since in pràctice associations mainly conclude civil law contracts with athletes, mutual rights and obligations largely depend on the content of

152. This list is up-to-date on 28 Feb. 2020: http://www.olympic.si/datoteke/PREGLED%20zaposlenih%20%C5%A1portnikov%20na%20MORS%20MNZ%20FURS-stanje%2028_2_2020%20(2).pdf (accessed 31 Jul. 2020).

an individual contract. These contracts do not have to be in writing to be valid. Oral agreements are also legally valid. The written form is intended primarily for the safety of the contracting parties, so that the content of the agreement can be determined subsequently. If any of the issues in the contract is not regulated, the rules of the law of obligations shall apply in this regard, either general or special, if the contract can be placed in one of the categories of contracts regulated by the Code of Obligations.[153] These rules also apply when the athlete and the association agree on something in the contract that is contrary to the cogent rules.

II. Private Regulation

203. Athletes enter into different legal relationships with their clubs and sport federations. The relationship with sport federations cannot relate only to athletes as competitors of sport clubs, but it can also relate to athletes as members of national teams.

A. *Legal Relationship Between Athletes and Clubs*

1. General Issues

204. Sometimes autonomous rules of sport federations prescribe that contracts must be concluded in writing and the components (such as duration of the contract, compensation that an athlete receives) that must be included in a contract between athletes and clubs. These requirements often depend on the status of the athlete according to federations' rules. Athletes are usually divided into two groups: amateurs and professionals. The rules of the latter group are usually stricter. We note that the definitions of amateurs and professionals differ from federation to federation. Failure to comply with these requirements does not affect the legal validity of contracts, but can have an effect only within such an organization (e.g., club cannot register a player, because the contract does not have all elements that are mandatory according to autonomous rules of certain sport federation). Besides that, clubs can receive disciplinary sanctioned by the federation for not complying with its autonomous rules.

2. Football Association of Slovenia

205. Regulation on the registration and status of players do not regulate contracts between clubs and amateur players. Therefore, the conclusion of a written contract and its content between the amateur player and the club is entirely left to their will. However, since the club cannot register an (amateur) player if the latter

153. Official Journal of the Republic of Slovenia, No. 97/07 (Official Consolidated Text).

does not give consent for registration, it can be said that already giving consent for registration represents the establishment of a contractual relationship between the club and the athlete.

206. On the other hand, this regulation stipulates that a professional football player must have a written contract with the club in the form of a unified football contract. Contracts between professionals and clubs must include a provision on duration of the contract and obligations of contractual parties. If a player's licensed agent has participated in the conclusion of the contract, his name must be specified in the contract. The contract must also be according to valid other rules of Slovenian Football Association, FIFA rules and other Slovenian public regulations. Players younger than 15 years are not allowed to conclude professional contracts. Players between 15 and 18 years can conclude professional contracts, but only for a period that is not longer than three years and with a signature of player's legal representative (usually parents). Regulations state that the contract (and its changes or updates) must be concluded in writing. A copy of the written contract and its possible changes and updates must be sent to the registration authority of Slovenian Football Association, otherwise the club can be liable for disciplinary sanctions.

3. Ski Association of Slovenia

207. Ski Association of Slovenia does not have rules regarding the form in which contracts among clubs and athletes have to be concluded. The same goes for the content of these contracts. Unlike Slovenian Football Association this federation also does not divide athletes into amateurs and professionals. Since competitors are primarily not clubs, but athletes themselves, as skiing is an individual sport, skiers have the right to compete in all competitions even if they are not members of ski clubs, but they have to be direct members of Slovenian Ski Association.[154] Exceptions are made for foreigners, who do not receive championship points.

208. Nevertheless, Slovenian Ski Association has adopted Rules on the Registration of competitors.[155] These rules, of course, only apply to those skiers that are registered for certain clubs. These rules mention the word 'contract' only in connection with compensation that a skier has to pay to his (former) club if he wishes to register for another club. Ski club is entitled to the compensation only if he has concluded a (written)[156] contract. In this case ski club can condition the issue of transfer document with the payment of compensation. Of course, ski club and athletes

154. These are so-called extraordinary members. We believe that this membership is contrary to the Societies Act, since members of associations of societies can only be societies. Besides that articles of association forbids extraordinary members to participate in competition system, but other acts of Slovenian Ski Association allow extraordinary members to compete. Rules are therefore mutually inconsistent and inconsistent with the practice.

155. Available only in Slovenian language at: http://www.sloski.si/resources/files/pdf/Registracijski%2 0pravilnik09.pdf (accessed 31 Jul. 2020).

156. The word 'written' is not exactly stated in these Rules, but it can be assumed that it is meant so.

can also arrange other mutual rights and obligations with a written contract, if they choose to, but autonomous rules do not require from them to do so.

B. Legal Relationship Between Athletes and Sport Federations

1. General Issues

209. Athletes who are members of national teams have legal relationships with sport federations. Sport federations usually adopt rules that have to be followed by every national team member, but each athlete gives a special consent to follow these rules, so this is in fact a contractual relationship. Usual obligations of national team members are to:

- arrive to training and matches, when an athlete is chosen as a member of national team;
- train;
- follow the rules of conduct;
- use the national team equipment;
- follow anti-doping rules;
- participate in press conferences;
- participate on TV and radio as members of national teams; and
- be available to sponsors of national teams for photo shootings, recording of advertisements, etc.

210. Rights of national team members usually relate to reimbursement of costs that occur when he comes to the national team gathering, daily allowances, awards for the success, reimbursement of training costs if a member of national team trains by himself, insurance. As this legal relation is a contractual one, an individual relation can sometimes differ from rules of sport federations (especially if an athlete is indispensable for the national team and has a strong negotiating position).

211. Instructions that relate to trainings and matches are given to athletes by the selector who also decides who will become a member of national team. It is not unusual that rules regarding trainings are individually negotiated if a member of national team is injured or tired.

2. Football Association of Slovenia

212. Slovenian Football Association adopted the Rules on Slovenian national football teams.[157] These rules apply not only to athletes but also to other members of national teams (selector, trainers, doctors, physiotherapists, etc.) as well. Rights

157. Available only in Slovenian language at: https://www.nzs.si/Doc/Arhiv/Predpisi%20NZS/PRAVILNIK_NZS_O_REPREZENTANCAH_.pdf (accessed 31 Jul. 2020).

and obligations of other members of national teams are not always the same as rights and obligations of athletes. In this section, we will only discuss those that relate to athletes.

213. Legal relationship between football players and Slovenian Football Federation is concluded when an athlete signs a statement annexed to the Rules. This statement is as follows:

> I, the undersigned, X. Y., hereby declare that I am aware of the rights and obligations stated in Rules on Slovenian national football teams, adopted by Slovenian football Association, in particular as regards obligation to respond to the call, rules of conduct and dress, use of equipment, the rules on remuneration, with I agree, and I assure them that I will be fully respected.

214. Obligations of athletes (football players) according to the above-mentioned rules are:

- to respond to the official call of national team selector and to play for national team;
- to follow the Articles of Association of Slovenian Football Association, different rules, instructions and other acts of Slovenian Football Association, UEFA and FIFA, and not to use doping substances;
- to attend group or individual audio or video recordings, photo shootings, public events and other media events required by sponsors or partners of Slovenian Football Association;
- to attend press conferences and TV broadcasts when they are part of national teams;
- members of national teams can decide for themselves whether or not to make statements outside of press conferences, but they can make statements only in the scenic background of the Slovenian Football Association, if it is raised;
- when giving statement, members of national teams are obliged to respect the fundamental principles of the Slovenian Football Association, as defined by its articles of association;
- football players transfer the economic exploitation of their image rights to Slovenian Football Association in connection to national teams;
- to behave properly in time of national team gathering (loyalty, integrity, sportsmanship, not to be politically and religiously active, not do discriminate, etc.);
- to dress in clothes provided by Slovenian Football Association and to return these clothes when national team gathering ends.

215. Violation of these obligations can be sanctioned by disciplinary sanctions which can be monetary or other (warning, exclusion from the national team, etc.).

216. According to the rules, rights of football players are entitled to:

- reimbursement of travel expenses for arrival to national teams' gatherings;

- payment of daily allowances in periods when they are part of national team (only members of national team A and U-21 players);
- payment of insurance premiums for accident insurance;
- payment of monetary awards in case of a win or a draw for every game and special award for participating in European championship or World cup (only members of national team A);
- payment for their commercial image right exploitation by Slovenian Football Association (only members of national team A);
- payment of awards for newly concluded sponsorship contracts by Slovenian Football Association because national team has qualified for European championship or world cup (only members of national team A); and
- additional special prizes for good sporting results (only members of national team A).

3. Ski Association of Slovenia

217. For every ski discipline Slovenian Ski Association has adopted rules on the rights and obligations of national team competitors. Since these rules do not differ much between ski disciplines, we will only describe the content of these rules for alpine skiing.

218. Rules on rights and obligations of alpine skiing national team's competitors[158] state that each national team competitor has to conclude a contract with Slovenian Ski Association, with which he acquires rights and take over obligations under these rules. Both contractual parties can arrange their legal relationship in a way that differs from such rules.

219. According to these rules, skiers, who are members of national team, are obliged to:

- carry out all activities in Slovenia and abroad undertaken by Slovenian Ski Association, which are pre-agreed or pre-booked (trainings, preparations, testing, competitions);
- participate on all training sessions (fitness and snow) programme of work;
- participate in all tests and medical examinations;
- lead a lifestyle of an athlete (resting, non-consummation of alcohol, nicotine and drugs, etc.);
- participate in all international competitions in the adopted programme;
- participate at the annual national championship;
- participate in all domestic FIS competitions if they are part of the adopted programme;
- comply with all rules of Slovenian Ski Association and FIS;

---

158. Available only in Slovenian language at: https://www.sloski.si/resources/files/pdf/alpsko-smucanje/2021/Pravilnik_o_pravicah_in_dolznostih_tekmovalcev_pAS.pdf (accessed 31 Jul. 2020).

- attend all press conferences, receptions and other events, organized by Slovenian Ski Association;
- attend the announcement of the results;
- not engage in hazardous activities that could cause injury or damage health, so that the athlete could not train and compete;
- act in public in a manner to promote Slovenian Ski Association and skiing in general;
- not compete in other competitions, except for their clubs or if its otherwise allowed in writing by Slovenian Ski Association;
- respect the rules of the Charter of the IOC and OCS, in particular the rules against doping and to participate in doping verification procedures;
- comply with tax rules;
- transfer the economic exploitation of their image rights to Slovenian Ski Association;
- comply with strict sponsorship rules;
- inform Slovenian Ski Association that he plans to conclude a contract to use a vehicle under which he will be able to use a vehicle;
- contribute to the costs of training in the amount determined by the contract;
- use the equipment, provided by Slovenian Ski Association, to take care of this equipment, etc.; and
- conclude insurance contracts for injuries at his own expense.

220. If a skier does not follow these obligations he can be monetarily or otherwise (prohibition of competition, exclusion from the national team, etc.) disciplinarily sanctioned.

221. On the other hand, the rules state that skiers, who are members of national team, have the right to:

- be informed on time about the short-term, medium-term and long-term programme of work, in order to organize their schedule;
- receive some of the sponsorship income of the Slovenian Ski Association;
- conclude a sponsorship contract with one personal sponsor whose name can be on the national team clothes; in case if a skier has a special championship status,[159] he can have up to five sponsors; in any case personal sponsors cannot compete in the market with sponsors of Slovenian Ski Association;
- receive a skiing equipment (skies, clothes, helmets, etc.) from Slovenian Ski Association for free usage; and

159. Such status has a skier that was either:

- on the podium in total ranking of FIS World Cup;
- the first in common in the sum of the individual disciplines of the World Cup;
- on the podium at the World Championships; and
- on the podium at Olympics.

– those skiers that have a championship status have the right to form their own team, and if they realize this, they have the right to receive a compensation for training from Slovenian Ski Association.

§4. Agents' Regulation

I. Public Regulation

222. The principle of contractual autonomy applies in Slovenian contract law, but it is not without restrictions. Article 3 of the Code of Obligations prescribes that participants are free to regulate obligations, but may not regulate them contrary to the Constitution, coercive regulations or moral principles. The Sports Act has no provisions on sports agents and the same applies to other legislations. This means that only the rules of the Code of Obligations apply to these issues. These are mainly general rules, but depending on the content of the contract concluded by the sports agent, the provisions on the brokerage contract (Articles 837–850 of the Code of Obligations) and the agency contract (Articles 807–836 of the Code of Obligations) may also apply if the contract does not explicitly regulate certain issues.[160] The main difference between the two contracts is in the authorization of the broker or agent.[161] Unlike an agent, the broker does not enter into a contract in the name and on behalf of the represented.

II. Private Regulation

223. Although sports law does not restrict contractual freedom, this does not mean that agents who want to work in a particular sport are always completely free in their work. The same goes for athletes and sports clubs. In some sports, the autonomous rules of sports organizations prescribe restrictions on contractual freedom and performance. Athletes, sports clubs and agents must commit to following these rules if they want to operate in a particular sport.

A. Football Association of Slovenia

224. The Football Association's rules on agents are extensive. This Association has adopted a special regulation of player agents.[162] The naming is not entirely appropriate, as its content shows that it regulates not only the agents of the players but also the agents of the clubs. The purpose of adopting the rules is to increase the

160. Cf. conclusion of the Supreme Court of Slovenia II Ips 226/2012 of 15 Sep. 2014.
161. M. Đorđević, *Pogodba o trgovskem zastopanju (zastopniška pogodba)*, 222 (N. Plavšak ed., *Gospodarske pogodbe*, Book 2, Gospodarski vestnik 1994).
162. Available only in Slovenian language at: https://www.nzs.si/Doc/Arhiv/Predpisi%20NZS/Pravilnik_o_agentih_igralcev.pdf (accessed 3 Aug. 2020).

quality of services provided by agents and prevent abuse through appropriate education and supervision. The provisions of the regulation apply only to the activity of agents who, for the purpose of concluding or re-concluding a football contract, connect a player with a club or, for concluding a transfer agreement, connect two clubs. For other services provided by agents, although this may be related to players or clubs, the policy does not apply.

225. As a rule, football players and football clubs may only hire licensed agents for representation services relating to the conclusion of a contract or transfer. The regulation prescribes some exceptions to this rule. The first is that some family members (parents, siblings and spouses) are allowed to represent the footballer in concluding a playing contract. Attorneys may represent players or clubs if they notify the Football Association beforehand. We will no longer deal with exceptions in the following.

226. The Football Association of Slovenia is competent for issuing a licence for Slovenian citizens or for those who are not otherwise Slovenian citizens if they have resided in Slovenia for at least two years. Other persons must obtain a licence from other national football associations. To obtain a licence, a person must apply in writing. The conditions for obtaining a licence are met only by a natural person who has a reputation in the society. An individual is considered to enjoy a reputation if he has not been convicted of an economic crime or of an element of violence. Likewise, an agent cannot be someone who has a particular position in a club or affiliated clubs, be it nationally or internationally. By submitting the application, the person agrees to abide by the autonomous football sports rules. After submitting the application, the Football Association of Slovenia invites the candidate to take an exam in knowledge of football regulations, which mainly relate to transfers, and civil law regulations (personality rights and contract law). The candidate who passes the exam must then take out insurance with the insurance company in Slovenia for damage that could occur in the course of his activity, or he must submit a bank guarantee in the amount of at least CHF 100,000. The candidate is also obliged to sign the code of professional ethics, which is an integral part of the rules.

227. Only when all these conditions are met, the Football Association of Slovenia grants the candidate a licence that is personal in nature and not transferable. This licence enables the candidate to perform his/her activity in organized football all over the world, and he/she must comply with the legislation of Slovenia and the legislation of the country where he/she performs his/her activity. The licence is valid for five years and can be renewed, but the person must retake the exam. However, the licence may also be terminated before that time if the person no longer meets the conditions or ceases to carry out the activity.

228. The regulation further regulates the rights and obligations of agents, football players and clubs regarding representation in the conclusion of contracts and transfers of players between clubs. Agents must enter into a written contract with a football player or football club. The contract is valid for a maximum of two years and can be extended by explicit agreement. It must contain information about the clients, the period of validity of the contract, payment for the agent, method of payment, date of conclusion and signatures of the clients. The conclusion of a contract does not affect the footballer's right to conclude a playing contract. Payment must be agreed in the form of a percentage of the footballer's gross income. The rules also contain a model contract, which is not mandatory, but only recommended. An agent may contact a player who is in a contractual relationship with another agent, but may not convince him that he is in breach of the playing contract. Agents must also not act in contravention of regulations in the Republic of Slovenia and autonomous football sports rules and have to obey the code of professional ethics. Footballers may only authorize agents who are licensed or a person covered by the above exceptions. The contracts must state the agent's name. If the footballer does not use the services of an agent, this must be written in the contract. Clubs can enter into contracts and arrange player transfers through agents. They must be licensed, except in the case of the exceptions provided for. Contracts concluded by clubs must state the name of the agent, if this was concluded through his mediation, or it must be stated that the agent did not participate in the conclusion of the contract. An independent and impartial arbitral tribunal shall settle disputes arising in connection with the activity of agents.

229. The regulation also prescribes various sanctions for agents, football clubs and footballers if they violate it. These sanctions take the form of warnings, fines, suspensions, revocations of licences, revocation of competition points, bans on appearances, bans on transfers, transfers to a lower level of competition and even a ban on further participation in football-related activities. The Football Association of Slovenia or its bodies imposes these penalties.

B. *Ski Association of Slovenia*

230. The Ski Association of Slovenia does not have internal rules on agents, so athletes, clubs and agents can conclude any contracts that are in accordance with public regulation.

§5. Employment and Economic Dispute Settlements

I. Public Regulation

231. Irrespective of whether an employment contract or a civil law contract has been concluded with the athlete, state bodies, as a rule of courts, are primarily intended for resolving disputes. Self-help is forbidden. If the athlete and the sport organization have concluded an employment contract or the athlete claims that there is an employment relationship between them, but employment contract has not been concluded, a specialized labour court is competent to resolve these individual labour disputes. Otherwise, courts of general jurisdiction are competent to resolve disputes between athletes and organizations that they cannot resolve by themselves.

A. Employment Disputes

232. Mainly the Labour and Social Courts Act[163] prescribe the rules of procedure. Article 23 of the mentioned Act states that a law or a collective agreement may provide for a compulsory procedure for the amicable settlement of disputes. In such a case, the court has jurisdiction to resolve disputes only if such proceedings have been initiated but have not been successfully concluded within thirty days of its commencement. However, these provisions shall not apply in disputes concerning the existence or termination of employment. These rules therefore do not prevent the courts from deciding on individual labour disputes, but merely postpone decision-making to a later date if the employee and the employer fail to reach an agreement. It is important to note that it is only the law or the collective agreement that can set such a restriction, which means that autonomous rules of sports organizations or a contractual agreement are not sufficient.

233. Important for this monograph is the question of whether the resolution of labour disputes can be left entirely to another body. It would be unconstitutional for a law, collective agreement or other general act to stipulate as obligatory that disputes are not resolved before courts but before other tribunals.[164] Only with the consent of both parties can the jurisdiction of the court be excluded.[165] Due to the subordination of the employee in relation to the employer, the Employment Relationships Act prescribes the conditions for such an agreement in Article 201. Such a way of resolving disputes must be provided for in a collective agreement, which is binding on the employee and the employer. However, this is not enough to exclude judicial protection. This must be specifically agreed between the employee and the employer, and such an agreement is only possible after the dispute has already arisen. If such an agreement had been concluded earlier (e.g., in an employment contract), it would have been invalid.[166] The conclusion of a valid arbitration agreement results in the waiver of the judicial settlement of disputes, but this only applies if the arbitral tribunal decides quickly. Namely, the Act stipulates that if the arbitral tribunal does not decide within the time limit set by the collective agreement, but no later than ninety days, the employee may request judicial protection before the court. The jurisdiction of the arbitral tribunal may be agreed between the employee and the employer on those disputes which enable settlement, which also includes disputes concerning the existence and termination of the employment relationship.[167]

234. The settlement of economic disputes is better known in the Slovenian system as the resolution of collective labour disputes of interest. These must be clearly

163. Official Journal of the Republic of Slovenia, Nos 2/04, 10/04, 45/08, 45/08, 47/10, 43/12 and 10/17.
164. A. Galič, *A Commentary of Article 23*, 122–123 (J. Novak ed., *Zakon o delovnih in socialnih sodiščih s komentarjem,* GV Založba 2005).
165. J. Novak, *Delovni spori*, 241 (GV Založba 2004).
166. K. Kresal Šoltes, *A Commentary of Article 201*, 1065 (N. Belopavlovič, B. Kresal, K. Kresal Šoltes & D. Senčur Peček eds, *Zakon o delovnih razmerjih s komentarjem*, GV Založba 2016).
167. *Ibid.*, 1066.

distinguished from other types of collective labour disputes, which are disputes over rights. It is characteristic of interest (economic) collective labour disputes that they are resolved out of court. The subject of interest disputes is the amendment, supplementation or conclusion of a new collective agreement or withdrawal from it.[168] In this sense, a special Collective agreements Act[169] defines a dispute of interest.

235. The parties to a collective agreement are the trade union or their association and the employer or their association. There are two sports-related unions in Slovenia, namely the Slovenian Athletes' Union and the Professional Football Players' Union. None of them has enough members to obtain the status of a representative trade union under the Representativeness of Trade Unions Act.[170] This is not an obstacle to not concluding a collective agreement, but at the time of writing this monograph in Slovenia there is no collective agreement for sports, individual sports or for individual sport clubs. Even if a representative trade union succeeded in concluding a collective agreement, it would apply only to the members of that trade union and not to all athletes (in a particular sport). Such an effect would only have a collective agreement concluded by a representative trade union.

B. Other Disputes

236. In the absence of labour disputes, disputes shall be settled by courts of general jurisdiction. If the disputes are of a property nature or are such that the parties can settle the claim, they may conclude an arbitration agreement on them. It is an agreement that requires the parties to submit to arbitration for the resolution of all or certain disputes that have already arisen or may arise in connection with a particular legal relationship. The arbitration agreement must be concluded in writing. If an action is brought before a court in a case, which is the subject of an arbitration agreement, the court may not rule on the case, as it has no jurisdiction over it. The defendant must challenge jurisdiction.

C. Athlete Ombudsman

237. Article 66 of the Sports Act provides for an interesting legal institute that can contribute to resolving disputes. Its main tasks include dealing with complaints from athletes and sports organizations (e.g., clubs). It works without the possibility of decision-making. The ombudsman does his job unprofessionally. In his work, he is independent and autonomous and acts honourably, honestly and in good faith. He may address suggestions, changes, criticisms or recommendations to athletes and sports clubs, which they are obliged to consider and respond to within the deadline set by the ombudsman himself, which may not be shorter than eight days. In order to be able to perform his tasks, he is entitled to require the holders to provide him

168. J. Novak, *Delovni spori*, 355 (GV Založba 2004).
169. Official Journal of the Republic of Slovenia, Nos 43/06 and 45/08.
170. Official Journal of the Republic of Slovenia, No. 13/93.

with the information, which they are obliged to provide to him no later than five days from the receipt of the request. In the case of the athlete's personal data, the ombudsman may only obtain the data if the athlete consents.

238. The ombudsman is appointed by the Government, which is also obliged to provide him with the conditions for performing his function (premises, equipment, etc.). He is entitled to remuneration for his work and to reimbursement of expenses incurred in this connection. The former high jumper Rožle Prezelj currently performs the work of the ombudsman.

II. Private Regulation

239. Sports organizations often include clauses in their autonomous rules that exclude the jurisdiction of state and supranational courts to resolve disputes. Instead, they anticipate that arbitral tribunals that specialize in sports issues resolve disputes. Agreeing to such a clause is a necessary condition if the athlete wishes to compete within a particular sports organization. In this case we can talk about so-called forced arbitration clauses,[171] which, however, are not in themselves due to this kind of coercion. If a party has consented to the jurisdiction of the arbitral tribunal, even though that consent was strictly necessary to enable it to compete, such clause is lawful. However, for the decision of the arbitral tribunal to be lawful, the procedure must be fair. Of course, such consent is not relevant if the parties agreed to settle the dispute before arbitration, even if this would be contrary to public order.

A. Football Association of Slovenia

240. According to the provisions of the statute, regional associations of football clubs wishing to join the Slovenian Football Association must agree to an arbitration clause. These associations must also ensure that their members (i.e., football clubs) agree to an arbitration clause. Furthermore, football clubs must ensure that their members (footballers) agree that disputes between them are resolved before arbitration. In all cases, the arbitration clause is valid if it is in accordance with the legal order of the Republic of Slovenia.

241. Within the Football Association, a permanent arbitration is established, which is competent for resolving disputes with the national element. Details of the organization, composition and procedure are set out in the Arbitration Regulation.[172] This arbitration provides for a single-stage decision. It is also competent to decide on disputes arising from the contractual relationship between football clubs and players, unless the disputes involve participants belonging to different national

171. Cf. V. Bergant Rakočević, *Reševanje sporov pred Arbitražnim sodiščem za šport (CAS)*, 381–381 (V. Bergant Rakočević ed., *Šport in pravo*, Inštitut za lokalno samoupravo in javna naročila 2020).
172. Available only in Slovenian language at: https://www.nzs.si/Doc/Pravilnik%20o%20Arbitra%C5%BEi_V2.0._19062019.pdf (accessed 6 Aug. 2020).

football associations. Footballers and clubs are obliged to resolve these disputes exclusively before the arbitration and respect its decisions. The Rules on Arbitration define in great detail the composition of the arbitration, the course of the proceedings and the decision. We do not describe this, as a detailed discussion of this content would go beyond the purpose of this monograph.

B. *Ski Association of Slovenia*

242. The Ski Association of Slovenia does not envisage in its general acts that disputes between it and athletes (e.g., competitors) be resolved out of court. Such a provision may otherwise be contained in an individual contract concluded with a competitor. However, there is no body within the Ski Association to deal with these disputes, so at most it would be possible to set up an ad hoc arbitration.

§6. Social Security

I. General Issues

243. As a rule, an individual acquires the status of an insured person independently of his/her will, when the prescribed conditions for inclusion in social insurance are met. According to the provisions of the Sports Act, these are the conclusion of an employment contract or the commencement of activities as a self-employed person (a professional athlete). These cases include health insurance, pension and disability insurance, unemployment insurance and parental insurance. However, the regulations stipulate another form of compulsory insurance, which applies only to health and pension and disability insurance. If an athlete earns income under a civil law contract, but neither in the context of employment nor in the course of self-employment, health insurance contributions and pension and disability insurance contributions must be paid from the income received.[173] The amount of these contributions and thus the scope of insurance in these cases are different from that of 'regular' insurance within the framework of an employment relationship or self-employment.

244. So far, we have dealt with regular insurance bases that apply to both athletes and other persons. However, there are two other independent legal bases for insurance, which only concern persons with the status of a top athlete under the Sports Act. If a person acquires the status of a top athlete and is not insured on another basis, he or she must be insured as a top athlete. The profession estimates that this insurance basis is unnecessary.[174] Athletes are also insured for injuries at work and disability and death resulting from an injury at work if they participate in a sporting activity or action (e.g., a sports match).

173. G. Strban in L. Mišič, *Socialne pravice športnikov in trenerjev*, 192 (V. Bergant Rakočević ed., *Šport in pravo*, Inštitut za lokalno samoupravo in javna naročila 2020).
174. *Ibid.*, 193.

245. The rights deriving from the insurance bases just discussed depend on the type of insurance. Health insurance guarantees the right to health services (medical examinations, treatment services and cash benefits). Pension and disability insurance guarantees the right to an old age and disability pension. Unemployment insurance guarantees the right to cash benefits for a certain period of unemployment. Parental care insurance guarantees the right to maternity and paternity leave, the right to parental leave, the right to work part-time and the payment of social security contributions due to parenthood. In some cases, the regulations give athletes some additional rights compared to other policyholders (e.g., the right to a preventive medical examination).

II. Bridging Insurance for Athletes

246. Slovenia enacted Bridging Insurance of Professional and Top Athletes Act[175] which aims to provide professional and top athletes with social security after the end of their careers. This objective is ensured either by the payment of bridging annuities in monthly amounts or by a one-off cash payment for value of the assets entered in the personal account of the insured.[176] Bridging insurance is compulsory for professional[177] athletes employed by a sports association that is a member of a national trade union federation or a national branch sport federation. Top athletes who have permanent residence in Slovenia can join the insurance voluntarily. In Slovenia, clubs do generally not employ athletes, and they do not opt for this form of insurance voluntarily. That is the reason that bridging insurance did not come to life. As there were no policyholders, the insurance fund was automatically liquidated on 30 June 2018. The law is still in force, but it is not being implemented, even though favourable tax relief is provided to encourage access to insurance.[178]

III. Supplement to the Pension for Work and Outstanding Achievements in the Field of Sports

247. Act Regulating the Supplement to Pensions for Work and Outstanding Achievements in Sports[179] states that the beneficiary of the supplement to the pension is a citizen of the Republic of Slovenia who has made a lasting contribution to the development of society and the reputation of the Republic of Slovenia through

175. Official Journal of the Republic of Slovenia, No. 82/15.
176. G. Strban in L. Mišič, *Socialne pravice športnikov in trenerjev*, 205 (V. Bergant Rakočević ed., *Šport in parvo*, Inštitut za lokalno samoupravo in javna naročila 2020).
177. This law conceives a professional athlete differently from the Sports Act. Namely, a professional athlete is a person who has an employment contract and is employed as an athlete in the Republic of Slovenia, or a person who is entered in the register of professional athletes and has the status of a professional athlete in accordance with the law governing sports. Under a civil contract he works as an athlete abroad.
178. Tax reliefs are shown in the next section of this monograph.
179. Official Journal of the Republic of Slovenia, No. 34/17.

work and outstanding achievements in the field of sports and is a pension beneficiary. Of course, the recipient of a pension supplement can only be one who already receives a pension on the basis of compulsory insurance, either under Slovenian regulations or under foreign regulations, if Slovenia has concluded an international agreement with this country in this field. The athlete who received an Olympic medal or a medal at the World Championships in Olympic Sports Disciplines in adult competition contributed an outstanding achievement. The same is true if an athlete receives the Bloudek[180] Lifetime Achievement Award or a top international sporting achievement. An athlete receives this prize under Article 5.3 and 5.4 of the Bloudek Awards Act.[181] Irrespective of their achievements, those athletes who have been punished under doping rules and those who have been legally sentenced to imprisonment for more than six months are not entitled to the allowance. The supplement is granted to a former athlete according to the pension he receives, so that he can receive the highest maximum pension in Slovenia for forty years of service. The supplement amounts to a minimum of 70% and a maximum of 100% of the difference, depending on the type and number of medals or awards received.

§7. Tax Law (Tax Status of Athletes)

I. Personal Income Tax Act

248. Individuals (natural persons) are taxable persons under Personal Income Tax Act.[182] Taxable persons are either residents or non-residents. Residents are liable to pay income tax on all income which source is in Slovenia and from all income, which source is outside Slovenia. Non-residents are liable to pay income tax on all income that has a source in Slovenia. Categories of income under Personal Income Tax Act are employment income, business income, agricultural and forestry activities income, income from renting property and transfer of property rights, capital income and other income. From athletes' perspective employment, business and other income are relevant.

A. Employment Income

249. Employment income is every income that originates from a subordinate contractual relationship regardless of the nature of the work. The taxation of income

180. The award was named after Stanko Bloudek (11 Feb. 1890 – 29 Nov. 1959) who was a Slovenian aeroplane and automobile designer, a sportsman and a sport inventor, designer, builder and educator. For details about his achievements, *see* https://en.wikipedia.org/wiki/Stanko_Bloudek (accessed 6 Aug. 2020).

181. Official Journal of the Republic of Slovenia, No. 112/05.

182. For a more detailed explanation, *see* J. Podlipnik, *Obdavčitev dohodkov športnikov* (Master Thesis, Law faculty in Maribor 2006).

that originates from a legal relationship that is not subordinate is also taxed as employment income as long as this income cannot be considered as business income.[183]

250. Employment income is mostly paid by sport clubs to athletes in collective sport disciplines. For income to be considered employment income, it is not important that a sport club and an athlete have concluded an employment contract. However, as we have already explained above, it is common in Slovenia that sport clubs do not employ athletes and this, at least in practise, influences tax status of income received from clubs. Therefore, in practise, irrespective that players (athletes) receive income that comes from subordinate legal relationship, clubs and athletes consider this income as business income, since players (athletes) have statuses of sole entrepreneurs or professional sportsmen. We have not yet noticed that Slovenian financial (tax) administration would problematize this behaviour, although we find it controversial.

B. Business Income

251. Income derived from independent professional services, regardless of the purpose and results of that activity is business income. Tax base of business income can be calculated either on the basis of actual revenue and expenditure or on the basis of actual revenue and flat rate expenditure of 80% of the revenue. Those taxpayers that have no more than EUR 50,000 business revenue per annum can use flat rate expenses calculation of tax base. For those taxpayers that pay full insurance contributions for at least one person, this threshold is raised to EUR 100,000 per annum. If a taxpayer chooses a flat rate expenses calculation of tax base, his income will not be included in a yearly tax base, but will be taxed separately with a 20% tax rate. We emphasize that flat rate taxation of business income is not available only to athletes, but to all natural persons that are perform business and fulfil the mentioned conditions.

252. But if an athlete chooses flat rate taxation instead of taxation using actual expenditure, he will not be able to use a special tax relief for those athletes that have a legal status of professional sportsman under Sports Act. Additional conditions to be able to use this tax relief are that such an athlete is not employed and is also not engaged in other activities. Those athletes that fulfil all these conditions can reduce their business income tax base in the amount of 15% of revenue annually and up to the amount of EUR 25,000. The maximum about of this tax relief is therefore EUR 3,750 annually.

183. This sort of income is occasional and not regular.

C. Other Income

253. Other income is any income that cannot be classified as employment income, business income, agricultural and forestry activities income, income from renting property and transfer of property rights or capital income or is not the income that is outside the scope of Personal Income Tax Act. Some examples of other income that are sometimes received by athletes are awards, donations, prizes (winnings) from competitions and scholarships (personnel and other).

254. Although awards are generally taxed as other income, this is not true for the awards for outstanding achievements in the (among others) field of sports if:

- they are paid by the state, local government or institution that is not a related person or a current, former or prospective employer of the recipient or a person who is associated with the recipient;
- they are not hidden payment for receivers regular income or income for work or services; and
- the recipient of award has been selected as the winner without his own activities or participation in the call log or in the process of selection.

Bloudek's prizes and Bloudek's plaques are among the sports prizes that are exempt from income tax under this provision.

255. Donations (gifts) can be classified as other income if they are given to athletes by a legal entity and a donation is not regarded as employment or business income. Donations received from individuals (natural persons) are not income according to Personal Income Tax Act, but they can be taxed according to Inheritance and Gift Taxation Act.

256. Prizes from competitions are other income as long as an athlete does not receive them from his club or he is not engaged in a business activity (e.g., a professional tennis or alpine skier player who is constantly competing in order to receive prizes).

257. Scholarships (personnel and other)[184] are not taxed if a receiver is a person who is a full-time pupil or student in Slovenia and the scholarship does not exceed minimum wage for a study in Slovenia or 160% minimum wage for a study abroad. If the scholarship exceeds this amount, only the surplus is taxed as other income.

258. In general, when an individual receives reimbursement of expenses withholding tax has to be paid. The taxpayer can claim back this withholding tax in his yearly tax return. An exception to the obligation of withholding is exists if reimbursement is made:

- for documented costs of transport, accommodation and per diem payment;

184. Another tax category of scholarships is the so-called governmental scholarships which are tax free.

– to an individual who is (among other situations) voluntarily or pursuant to an invitation participating in sports non-profit activities or in the non-profit activities of societies and their federations; and
– to an individual who receives only reimbursement of those costs and the reimbursement of cost is within prescribed limits (if an individual receives a fee plus reimbursement of the costs, withholding has to be paid on the whole amount that he receives).

D. Other Personal Income Tax Act Incentives Associated to Sport

259. A special tax exemption exists for cash prizes that Slovenia pays to the receivers of medals at Olympic Games, World, European and other international championships. This income is completely exempted from taxation according to Personal Income Tax Act.

II. Bridging Insurance of Professional and Top Athletes Act

260. Yet another income tax incentive for athletes is located Bridging Insurance of Professional and Top Athletes Act.[185] The purpose of this Act is to provide social security for professional and top athletes after completing an active sports career. Bridging insurance is based on payment of social security contributions for professional and top athletes, while the state provides tax incentives.

261. Articles 33 and 34 of the Act state that contributions paid for the bridging insurance of professional athletes are (up to certain amounts) not taxed when paid to the bridging fund (in case of employment income) or are considered as a tax deductible expense (in case of business income). These amounts are taxed when the athlete receives the money from a bridging fund either in monthly amounts or in lump sum payment. In both cases only a share of the received amount is taxable. In case of monthly amounts, this share is 30% of the payout and in case of lump sum payment 50% of the payout. The Act also stipulates that in the case of monthly amount payout such income is taxed as income from employment according to Personal Income Tax Act, and in the case of a lump sum, payout is taxed as other income according to Personal Income Tax Act. In my view, this provision is controversial, since in both cases it is the same type of income.

III. Inheritance and Gift Taxation Act

262. As it was already mentioned if an athlete receives a donation from another individual and this donation is not taxed as income, it can be taxed according to Inheritance and Gift Taxation Act. In short, monetary donations that are not received from close relatives and exceeding EUR 5,000 annually are taxable.

185. Official Journal of the Republic of Slovenia, No. 82/15.

IV. Value Added Tax Act

263. There are no special tax incentives in Value Added Tax Act that could be used by athletes. In order to be a taxable person an athlete must independently carry out any economic activity. Practising sport can, of course be an independent economic activity, but athletes who are 'employed' by their club are, at least regarding legal relationship to their club, not independent. If athletes' taxable turnover exceeds EUR 50,000 in a period of twelve months they are obliged to identify otherwise they are so-called small enterprises and can identity if they voluntarily choose to. Supplies of services made for consideration are typically athletes' taxable transactions (competing services,[186] sponsoring services, etc.). On the other hand, donations are outside of scope of VAT.

186. U. Kraßnig, *Taxable Event and Taxable Base for VAT of Artistes and Sportsmen under the Sixth Directive*, 457–458 (W. Loukota and M. Stefaner eds, *Taxation of Artistes and Sportsmen in International Tax Law*, Linde 2008).

Part III. Doping and Sport

Chapter 1. General Issues

264. It is assumed that doping is as old as competitive sport. Allegedly athletes in ancient Greece were using a variety of substances (such as different mushrooms, goat testicles) to help them achieve better sporting results. Doping cases with serious health problems and even fatalities have occurred at the end of the nineteenth century. Athletes were using substances such as alcohol, heroin, cocaine, strychnine. After the Second World War mainly amphetamine and in 1990s anabolic-androgenic steroids were used for doping. In the second half of the twentieth century, first doping cases were discovered in the Olympic Games, and the first disqualified athlete from these games was Ben Johnson in 1988.[187] Since then doping testing has been an important element of all major sporting events.

265. Although doping raises a lot of questions from philosophical-ethical, sociological, psychological, pharmacological, medical and economic point of view, it is nevertheless also a legal phenomenon. Criminal law, disciplinary law and civil law sanctions can arise for athletes who are using doping and for those who helped them.

266. There are few reasons why doping should be prohibited, but on the other hand many are still arguing that athletes should be free to use substances in order to achieve better results or at least that doping rules should not be so strict as they are now. The reasons for prohibition of doping are the protection of health and life of athletes, fair play in sport competitions and sport ethics.[188] Each of these arguments has a contra argument, but at the moment arguments for prohibition prevail.

267. We will shortly describe Slovenian legal basis governing the issue of doping, in terms of both public law and private law perspective.

187. V. Bergant Rakočević, *Doping*, 310–311 (V. Bergant Rakočević ed., *Šport & parvo*, GV Založba 2008).
188. Cf. J. Dvoršak, B. Koritnik & I. Angelovski, *Preprečevanje dopinga v športu*, 283 (V. Bergant Rakočević ed., *Šport in pravo*, Inštitut za lokalno samoupravo in javna naročila 2020).

Chapter 2. Public Regulation

§1. Constitutional Provisions Related to Doping and Sport

I. Direct Application of International Treaties (Article 8)

268. Slovenian laws and regulations must comply with generally accepted principles of international law and with treaties that are binding on Slovenia. Ratified and published treaties shall be applied directly.[189] The second sentence is especially important for this part of the monograph as Slovenia is a legal successor of former Yugoslavia that has ratified and published an Anti-Doping Convention,[190] and also because Slovenia has ratified and published an International Convention against Doping in Sport.[191]

II. Protection of Human Personality and Dignity (Article 21(1))

269. Respect for human personality and dignity shall be guaranteed in criminal and all other legal proceedings, as well as during the deprivation of liberty and enforcement of punitive sanctions. This constitutional norm is also applicable to doping legal proceedings that are conducted by authorities laid down by the autonomous rules of sports organizations if, of course, these proceedings take place in Slovenia. We are specially emphasizing this provision because determination of the facts in the anti-doping procedures required interventions in the human personality (collection of blood, urine, etc.). These procedures must be conducted in a manner which least interferes with the human rights of athletes and with respect for their human dignity.

§2. International Treaties Valid in Slovenia on Doping and Sport

I. Anti-doping Convention

270. The aim of COE's Anti-Doping Convention[192] is the reduction and eventual elimination of doping in sport. With the ratification of the Convention, Slovenia has undertaken to fulfil its obligations in respect of:

189. It must be noted that direct application is not always possible. If, for example, the content of the norm prevents direct application, then, of course, such norm will need further enactment in domestic legislation. Direct applicability is the quality of legal norms contained in general legal acts and not general legal acts as such. Cf. V. Sancin, *Mednarodno pravo v hierarhiji pravnih virov EU in njenih članic*, 172 (Uradni list Republike Slovenije 2009).
190. But Slovenia has not signed and ratified Additional Protocol to the Anti-Doping Convention.
191. Act Ratifying the International Convention against Doping in Sport (Official Journal of the Republic of Slovenia, No. 15/07).
192. https://www.coe.int/en/web/conventions/full-list/-/conventions/rms/090000168007b0e0 (accessed 6 Aug. 2020).

- domestic coordination;
- adopting measures to restrict the availability and use of banned doping agents and methods;
- laboratories;
- education;
- cooperation with sports organizations on measures to be taken by them;
- international cooperation; and
- provision of information.

271. Anti-Doping Convention contains an annex with a list of prohibited substances and methods. Since pharmaceutical and chemical industries are constantly developing new substances and methods, the Convention sets up a special monitoring group whose purpose is, among others, to adopt the list of prohibited substances. This list has been amended twenty times since the adoption of the Convention. Last amendment entered into force on 1 January 2020.

II. International Convention Against Doping in Sport

272. On 29 October 2005, United Nations Educational, Scientific and Cultural Organization (UNESCO) adopted an International Convention against Doping in Sport. The content of this convention is extensive in comparison with Anti-Doping Convention, but in essence it has the same purpose: 'to promote the prevention of and fight against doping in sport, with a view to its elimination'.

273. With ratifying this Convention, Slovenia has committed to:

- adopt appropriate measures at the national and international levels which are consistent with the principles of the World Anti-Doping Code (WADC) adopted by the World Anti-Doping Agency (WADA) on 5 March 2003 at Copenhagen which is attached as Appendix 1 to this Convention;
- encourage all forms of international cooperation aimed at protecting athletes and ethics in sport and at sharing the results of research; and
- foster international cooperation between states parties and leading organizations in the fight against doping in sport, in particular with the WADA.

274. In abiding by the obligations contained in this Convention, Slovenia has undertaken to adopt appropriate measures, such as legislation, regulation, policies or administrative practices.

§3. Provisions of State Laws on Doping and Sport

I. Sports Act

275. Sports Act once mentions the word 'doping'. Article 5, which lists the general principles of operation in sport, also defines a principle that could be called the principle of ethics. According to this, moral and ethical values in the field of sports must be protected and strengthened, and unfair results (doping, manipulation of competitive results) must be avoided. Unlike the previously valid law, however, the current one no longer has a provision stating that non-compliance with international anti-doping rules constitutes an offence. However, this does not mean that the legislator wanted to reduce the importance of the fight against doping. Doping must be fought, especially in the context of sports organizations, and the state where it is a crime.

II. The Criminal Code

276. Slovenian Criminal Code[193] mentions doping in two Articles 186 and 187. These two articles do not criminalize athletes who enjoy illicit substances in order to achieve better sport results, but persons who make this enjoyment possible for athletes (sellers, manufacturers, keepers, transporters, etc.). Therefore, enjoying these substances is not a criminal act, but producing and distributing them is.

277. Article 186 criminalizes unlawful manufacture and trade of illicit substances in sport. According to this article:

- anybody who unlawfully manufactures, processes, sells or offers for sale substances, which are classified as illicit substances in sport, or whoever purchases, keeps or transports such substances with a view to resell them, can be sentenced to imprisonment for not less than one and not more than ten years;
- anybody who sells, offers for sale or hands out free of charge substances, which are classified as illicit substances in sport to a minor, mentally disabled person, person with a temporary mental disturbance, severe mental retardation or person who is in the rehabilitation, or if the offence is committed in educational institutions or in immediate vicinity thereof, in prisons, military units, public places or public events, or if the offence under previous point is committed by a civil servant, priest, doctor, social worker, teacher or educator and thereby exploits his position, or whoever in order to commit the mentioned offence uses minors can be sentenced to imprisonment between three and fifteen years;
- if an offence from previous two points is committed within a criminal organization for the committing of such criminal offences, or if the perpetrator of this offence organized a network of resellers or agents, the perpetrator can be sentenced to imprisonment between five and fifteen years;
- whoever without an authorization manufactures, purchases, possesses or furnishes other persons with the equipment, substances or precursors, which are to his knowledge intended for the manufacture of illicit substances in sport, can be sentenced to imprisonment for not less than six months and not more than five years; and

193. Official Journal of the Republic of Slovenia, Nos 50/12 (Official Consolidated Text), 6/16, 54/15, 38/16, 27/17, 23/20 and 91/20.

- illicit substances in sport and the means of their manufacture and means of transport with a specially adapted space for the transport and storage of drugs or illicit substances in sport are seized.

278. Article 187 criminalizes rendering opportunity for consumption of illicit substances in sport. This article states that:

- whoever solicits another person to use illegal doping substances or provides a person with these substances to be used by him or by a third person, or whoever provides a person with a place or other facility for the use of illicit substances in sport can be sentenced to imprisonment for not less than six months and not more than eight years;
- whoever commits the offence under previous point against several persons, a minor, mentally disabled person, person with a temporary mental disturbance, severe mental retardation or person who is in the rehabilitation, or if the offence is committed in educational institutions or in immediate vicinity thereof, in prisons, military units, public places or public events, or if the offence under previous point is committed by a civil servant, priest, doctor, social worker, teacher or educator, and thereby exploits his position, can be sentenced to imprisonment between one and twelve years; and
- illicit substances in sport and the tools for their consumption are seized.

279. Slovenian Criminal Code does not contain a list of illicit substances in sport. According to the decision of Slovenian Constitutional Court No. U-I-335/02 (25 March 2005), it is not against the principle of legality in criminal law (Article 28 of the Slovenian Constitution) if illicit substances are not expressly stated in Criminal Code.[194] Since Slovenia has ratified and published two international treaties with attached lists of prohibited substances, this arrangement is likely to comply with the Slovenian Constitution. We are not aware of a publicly published case where this legal issue regarding illicit substances in sport would be raised.[195]

---

194. For example, illegal drugs are listed in Decree on the scheduling of illicit drugs (Official Journal of the Republic of Slovenia, Nos 49/00, 8/01 – correction, 49/01, 78/02, 53/04, 122/07, 102/09, 95/10, 58/11, 62/13 and 45/14), but illicit substances in sport are not.

195. More about these two crimes, *see* M. Šepec, *A Commentary of Articles 186 and 187*, 175–231 (D. Korošec, K. Filipčič & S. Zdolšek, *Veliki znanstveni komentar posebnega dela kazenskega zakonika*, Book 2, Uradni list Republike Slovenije and Pravna fakulteta Univerze v Ljubljani, 2019).

Chapter 3. Private Regulation

§1. Slovenian Olympic Committee

I. Slovenian Anti-Doping Organisation

280. Slovenian Anti-Doping Organisation (SLOADO) is a private institution established by OCS in 2013. It is a successor of National Anti-Doping Organisation established in 1996 by OCS and Ministry for Education and Sport.

281. SLOADO is an organization whose responsibility is to implement in Slovenia the programme of prevention of doping in sport, which is based on the protection of the fundamental rights of athletes to train and compete in doping-free environment. This organization must ensure a coordinated and effective programme to combat doping in the discovery, rejection and prevention of doping in sport. The emphasis of SLOADO is on raising awareness of athletes and other participants in all forms of sport, in shaping national group for testing athletes out-of-competition and constant presence in competitions of national sport federations in order to perform tests in competitions and other activities defined by the International Convention against Doping in Sport.

282. The Republic of Slovenia funds SLOADO through the Annual Sports Programme, the Foundation for the Financing of Sports Organizations and OCS. To a lesser extent, SLOADO acquires funds for operation from other sources.

II. International Regulation

A. *World Anti-Doping Code*

283. WADC was signed by the OCS, but Slovenia is also bound to it because the WADC is an annex to the International Convention against Doping in Sport that was ratified and published by Slovenia. But it has to be noted that the Annex contains a 2003 version of the Code, but currently a 2019 version is applicable.

284. WADC is the fundamental and universal document upon which the World Anti-Doping Programme in sport is based. The purpose of the Code is to advance the anti-doping effort through universal harmonization of core anti-doping elements. It is intended to be specific enough to achieve complete harmonization on issues where uniformity is required, yet general enough in other areas to permit flexibility on how agreed-upon anti-doping principles are implemented.

285. WADC which supports the World Anti-Doping Programme has two purposes:

(1) to protect the athletes' fundamental right to participate in doping-free sport and thus promote health, fairness and equality for athletes worldwide; and

(2) to ensure harmonized, coordinated and effective anti-doping programmes at the international and national level with regard to detection, deterrence and prevention of doping.

286. WADC content consists of the following parts:

- Part One: Doping Control (Definition of Doping, Anti-doping Rule Violations, Proof of Doping, The Prohibited List, Testing, Analysis of Samples, Results Management, Right to a Fair Hearing, Automatic Disqualification of Individual Results, Sanctions on Individuals, Consequences to Teams, Sanctions against Sporting Bodies, Appeals, Confidentiality and Reporting, Clarification of Doping Control Responsibilities, Doping Control for Animals Competing in Sport, Statute of Limitations).
- Part Two: Education and Research (Education, Research).
- Part Three: Roles and Responsibilities (Additional Roles and Responsibilities of Signatories, Additional Roles and Responsibilities of Athletes and Other Persons, Involvement of Governments).
- Part Four: Acceptance, Compliance, Modification and Interpretation (Acceptance, Compliance and Modification, Interpretation of the Code, Transitional Provisions).
- Appendix: Definitions.

B. International Regulation

287. International regulations that SLOADO has to follow are:[196]

- International Conventions:
  - Johannesburg Declaration 2013;
  - European Convention against Doping in Sport;
  - Copenhagen Declaration on Anti-doping in Sport;
  - International Convention against Doping in Sport; and
  - Lausanne Declaration on Doping in Sport.
- Codes and international standards:
  - WADC;
  - International standards for testing and investigation;
  - International standards for therapeutic exemptions;
  - International standards for laboratories; and
  - List of Prohibited Substances and Procedures 2020.

196. https://www.sloado.si/kategorija/mednarodna-pravila-sportniki (accessed 6 Aug. 2020).

III. National Regulation

A. *SLOADO Anti-Doping Rules*

288. Consolidated 2015 version of SLOADO Anti-Doping Rules[197] is currently valid. All national sport federations must comply with these rules. They include compliance in either their articles of association or other rules. By this all participants (clubs and individual athletes) of the sporting events organized by these sport federations must follow the anti-doping rules. A mandate is given to SLOADO by sport federations to carry out doping controls and imposing sanctions when violations are detected.

289. The purposes of doping controls are ethical (to guarantee fair play in sports) and medical (to protect the health and life of athletes). In these rules doping is defined as:

- presence of a prohibited substance or its metabolites or markers in an athlete's sample;
- use or attempted use by an athlete of a prohibited substance or a prohibited method;
- refusing or failing without compelling justification to submit to sample collection after notification as authorized in SLOADO anti-doping rules, or otherwise evading sample collection;
- violation of requirements regarding athlete's availability for out-of-competition testing, including failure to file required whereabouts information and missed tests which are declared based on rules which comply with the international standard for testing; any combination of three missed tests and/or filing failures within an eighteen-month period as determined by SLOADO shall constitute an anti-doping rule violation;
- tampering or attempted tampering with any part of doping control;
- possession of prohibited substances and use prohibited methods;
- trafficking or attempted trafficking in any prohibited substance or prohibited method; and
- administration or attempted administration to any athlete in-competition of any prohibited method or prohibited substance, or administration or attempted administration to any athlete out-of-competition of any prohibited method or any prohibited substance that is prohibited out-of-competition, or assisting, encouraging, aiding, abetting, covering up or any other type of complicity involving an anti-doping rule violation or any attempted anti-doping rule violation.

290. Regarding the burden of proof SLOADO Anti-Doping Rules state that in general SLOADO has to prove that anti-doping rule violation has occurred with the standard of proof greater than a mere balance of probability but less than proof beyond a reasonable doubt. If athletes and others have to prove certain facts of the

197. Available only in Slovenian language at: https://issuu.com/sloado/docs/protidopin__ki_pravilnik_sloado_201 (accessed 6 Aug. 2020).

anti-doping case the proving standard is, in general, a balance of probability, except in certain cases especially provided in the Rules when higher burden of proof must be satisfied.

291. The list of illicit substances and methods is an integral part of the Rules. This list is constantly changing with the development of technology. SLOADO has to inform sport federations about changes in the list. In general a substance or a method that is newly included in the list of becomes illicit after three months after WADA publishes new list.

292. International standard for therapeutic use exemptions is also included in these Rules. Athletes with special documented medical conditions who need certain illicit substances or methods to be able to live normally can request a therapeutic use exemption. With this right athletes can use some substances and methods that cannot be used by other athletes. These therapeutic use exemptions are approved to athletes by SLOADO, but can be monitored and therefore taken away by WADA.

293. Provisions about testing, samples analysing and results management are also included in these Rules, but we believe that for this monograph disciplinary proceedings rules are more important. SLOADO management board appoints members of a SLOADO Disciplinary Commission. The main task of this Commission is to render decisions on violations of the doping rules. Disciplinary Commission initiates the procedure when, on the basis of testing, it is suspected that anti-doping rules have been violated. The Commission has the right to conduct the proceedings at its discretion, but must allow the alleged infringer to participate in the process and that he is aware of the allegations. Decisions of the Commission have to be in writing and have to be sent to parties of the proceedings, to WADA, to OCS and to national sport federation and to international sport federation in which the athlete or the club was competing. When an athlete has violated anti-doping rules, the Commission can, taking into account all the circumstances of the case, render one or more of next decisions:

- disqualification (athlete's results in a particular competition or event are invalidated, with all resulting consequences including forfeiture of any medals, points and prizes);
- ineligibility (athlete or other person is barred for a specified period of time from participating in any competition or other activity or funding); and
- provisional suspension (athlete or other person is barred temporarily from participating in any competition prior to the final decision at a hearing).

In team sports if more than two members of a team are found to have committed an anti-doping rule violation, the ruling body has the right to impose an appropriate sanction on the team (e.g., loss of championship points, disqualification from a competition or event, or other sanctions) in addition to any consequences imposed upon the individual athletes committing the anti-doping rule violation. But if OCS or national sport federation is the organizer of the competition or event such sanction is imposed by SLOADO. These Rules state that in general if SLOADO provisionally suspends such team, the event organizer must immediately execute this decision.

294. The decision of the Commission is not final and can be challenged by an appeal which does not suspense the decision unless appellate body decides otherwise. Persons entitled to file an appeal are:

- the athlete or other person who is the subject of the decision being appealed;
- the other party to the case in which the decision was rendered;
- the relevant international sport federation;
- SLOADO or national anti-doping organization of the person's country of residence or countries where the person is a national or licence holder;
- the IOC or International Paralympic Committee, as applicable, where the decision may have an effect in relation to the Olympic Games or Paralympic Games, including decisions affecting eligibility for the Olympic Games or Paralympic Games;
- OCS; and
- WADA.

SLOADO arbitrage is competent to decide on the appeal. Rules also contain how arbitrage proceedings are carried out and what kind of decisions can be brought. The arbitrage decisions are final and can in general not be challenged. If challenging of arbitrage decisions is allowed, CAS is competent to review the arbitrage decisions.

295. The Rules also contain provisions on:

- obligations of SLOADO to report to WADA about testing, therapeutically exceptions, etc.;
- informing the public about anti-doping procedures;
- protection of confidentiality of data relating to doping procedures;
- recognition of decisions of the various national anti-doping organizations;
- statute of limitations (after eight years have passed from the day that anti-doping rules have been violated, an anti-doping procedure cannot be launched);
- financing SLOADO; and
- certain other provisions concerning the validity and application of the Rules.

§2. Sport Federations

I. General Issues

296. National sport federations and consequently regional sport federations, clubs and athletes are bound to follow anti-doping rules if they are either members of OCS or if international sport federation, whose members they are, has committed to follow international (WADA)[198] or national (SLOADO) anti-doping rules.

297. As a member of IOC, OCS is bound to follow the valid anti-doping rules. In order to become a member of OCS, national sport federation has to either submit a written statement to follow these rules or their articles of association have to state that they will follow the valid anti-doping rules. Without such written guarantee national sport federation cannot become a member of OCS. It is not sufficient that national sport federation that is a member of OCS commits to follow anti-doping rules, but it must also follow these rules in practise. If it fails to do so, it can lose its membership in OCS.

298. It is not sufficient that members of OCS commit to follow and actually follows anti-doping rules must themselves, but they must ensure that their member (regional sport federations or sport clubs) and athletes that compete in events and competitions that they organize do the same.

II. Football Association of Slovenia

299. Slovenian Football Association is a member of OCS and a member of FIFA. Both of them have committed to follow WADA anti-doping rules. This national sport federation does not have its own rules which regional football associations, clubs and athletes would have to bind to in order to be able to become a member, to compete, to register, to acquire a licence, etc. But since Slovenian Football Association demands that each of them has to comply with all UEFA rules, clubs, regional sport associations and athletes have to follow UEFA anti-doping regulations,[199] which in essence do not differ from WADA and SLOADO rules.

III. Ski Association of Slovenia

300. Slovenian Ski Association has, as a member of OCS and FIS,[200] committed to follow WADC. This also goes for ski clubs that are members of national ski federation and competitors that are either registered for ski clubs or they are just competing in ski competitions. The registered skiers are bound to follow the anti-doping rules in general and others are bound to do so when they wish to participate in certain competition. Skiers who are members of national team are also bound to

198. A list of international sport organizations who directly signed WADC is available at: https://www.wada-ama.org/en/what-we-do/the-code/code-signatories (accessed 6 Aug. 2020).

199. https://www.uefa.com/MultimediaFiles/Download/AntiDoping/uefaorg/Anti-doping/02/56/30/77/2563077_DOWNLOAD.pdf (accessed 6 Aug. 2020).

200. https://assets.fis-ski.com/image/upload/v1567168343/fis-prod/assets/FIS_Anti-Doping_Rules_August_2019.pdf (accessed 6 Aug. 2020).

follow anti-doping rules as that is expressly stated in rules of national team competitors for each skiing discipline. But the purpose of this express statement is that if they violate anti-doping rules they can be disciplinary sanctioned (e.g., they can be excluded from national team).

Part IV. Sport and Commerce

Chapter 1. General Issues

301. Since ancient times it has been possible to make money out of sport. Organizers of sport competitions can sell admission, food, drinks, souvenirs or sell others the right to do so. Athletes and clubs can earn appearance money, wages, prizes, sponsorship, transfer fees, bribes, etc. Other participants like coaches, referees, officials, doctors, agents, etc. also have the opportunity to earn their living. Everybody has the opportunity to earn from sport betting.[201]

302. It is therefore obvious that such a view on commercial aspects in sport would be too broad for this monograph. We will deal with the issues of sport commerce according to the outline: media and television rights, sponsoring, merchandising and ownership of clubs.

201. For a short history on the way money is earned in sports, *see* T. Harris, *Sports – Almost Everything You Ever Wanted to Know,* 589–688 (Yellow Jersey Press 2007).

Chapter 2. Public Regulation

§1. Constitutional Provisions Related to Sport and Commerce

I. Intellectual Property Rights (Article 60)

303. The protection of copyright and other rights deriving from artistic, scientific, research and invention activities is guaranteed according to Article 60 of the Slovenian Constitution. This article protects so-called rights of intellectual property which are divided into two groups: copyright (and other rights) and the rights of intellectual property (the rights that protect inventions, trademarks, etc.). The latter are especially important for this monograph as sport federations, sport clubs and even sport leagues and competitions can be trademarks that are known worldwide and can therefore be economically exploited in order to raise financial revenue.

II. The Freedom of Economic Initiative (Article 74(1))

304. According to the Slovenian Constitution free economic initiative is guaranteed. This means that in general any commercial subject has the right to freely engage in commercial activities in order to achieve profit. Commercial subjects have the right to choose their own business partners. Although sport clubs and federations in Slovenia are non-profit organizations, this does not mean that they are not protected by this constitutional norm, since they have the right to almost freely[202] engage in business activities, but they are not allowed to distribute profits that arise from these business activities. Profits must be used for financing non-profit activities.

§2. Provisions of State Laws

I. Media and Television Rights

305. Organizing a sport event can have important commercial implications. These are directly related to the public interest in the event. Organizers of sports events have a number of opportunities to earn money by concluding sponsorship contracts, selling media right, selling tickets (entrance fees), selling different goods and services at the event if we just name the most common ones. Revenues from the sale of media and television rights in most sports already exceed revenues from ticket sales, which is the traditional type of revenue for sport clubs.[203]

---

202. As non-profit organizations they are not allowed to entirely engage in profit activities. Business activities must have a supplementary nature and must be connected to their main (non-profit) purpose.
203. V. Bergant Rakočević, *Radiodifuzne pravice prireditelja*, 257 (V. Bergant Rakočević ed., *Šport in pravo*, Inštitut za lokalno samoupravo in javna naročila, 2020).

306. According to Sports Act, sports events are either organized sporting events or competitions. Sports events can be either private or public. According to Public Gathering Act,[204] a sporting event is a public event if anybody can attend under the conditions set by the organizer. This means that if the organizer has chosen to sell entrance tickets, anybody can attend as long as one buys a ticket. Access to the event is of course limited by space.

307. Selling of broadcasting rights is one of the most important sources of revenue for sports events' organizers. Organizers of sports events have the exclusive right to allow or prohibit exploitation of the sports events with the transfer of picture and sound at a distance from the scene. This means that media (television, radio, internet, etc.) can only show sporting event if they have permission from the organizer.

308. As a rule, law does not regulate the rights of the organizer. It is therefore a contractual relationship. The subject of the organizer's rights is the event as such, but it is sometimes difficult to determine who the organizer is, as not only the organizer but also others are involved in the organization of a sports event. This can be easily illustrated in the case of a ski race, where the organizer of a particular race is FIS, but the ski race is carried out with the help of the national ski association and a local sport club. These three participants have to arrange their relationships with each other regarding the ski race.[205] Of course, the organizer must also agree with the media service providers. As a rule, these are contractual arrangements. Their content is sometimes also influenced by autonomous sports rules. But nonetheless televisions and other media have the right to record and play short extracts from the event that was recorded by the media that exclusively transmitted the event if the footage does not exceed ninety seconds.[206] The legal basis for this in Slovenia is Audiovisual Media Services Act.[207] This right is given to them because information about sports events is of public interest. The recording is allowed to be used only for the purposes of general information broadcasts and no later than the day after the end of the event.

II. Sponsoring

309. According to the Slovenian Code of Obligations, participants are free to regulate obligational relationships, but may not act in contravention of the Constitution, compulsory regulations (*ius cogens*) or moral principles (free regulation of

204. Official Journal of the Republic of Slovenia, No. 64/11 (Official Consolidated Text).
205. V. Bergant Rakočević, *Radiodifuzne pravice prireditelja*, 259–262 (V. Bergant Rakočević ed., *Šport in pravo*, Inštitut za lokalno samoupravo in javna naročila 2020).
206. On the EU level, such extracts are allowed by a Directive 2010/13/EU of the European Parliament and of the Council of 10 Mar. 2010 on the coordination of certain provisions laid down by law, regulation or administrative action in Member States concerning the provision of audiovisual media services (Audiovisual Media Services Directive).
207. Official Journal of the Republic of Slovenia, Nos 87/11 and 84/15.

obligational relationships). Participants may regulate their obligational relationships in a manner different to that set out in the present Code of Obligations unless the contrary follows from an individual provision of the present code or from the meaning of an individual provision (optional nature of legal provision in Code of Obligations).

310. Slovenian law does not regulate a sponsorship contract as a specific civil law contract. Sponsorship contracts are therefore so-called innominate contracts. Since these contracts are not enacted, they lack the official definition; on the other hand theoretical definitions differ from each other. Defined broadly sponsorship contract could be defined as:

> Any commercial agreement by which a sponsor, for mutual benefit of the sponsor and sponsored party, contractually provides financial or other support in order to establish an association between the sponsor's image, brands or products and a sponsorship property in return for rights to promote this association and/or for granting of certain agreed direct or indirect benefits.[208]

Contracts that are concluded for philanthropic reasons under which one party simply provides to the other party some kind of support without receiving something in return are not sponsorship contracts. These contracts are usually referred to as donations contracts.

311. In sports sponsor can choose who or what he wishes to sponsor between:

- sponsoring an athlete;
- sponsoring a sport club (a team)[209] or sport federation;[210]
- sponsoring an event[211] or competition organizer;
- sponsoring a media coverage of sporting event; and
- sponsoring a sport infrastructure.[212]

312. Legal theory lists these elements that should be included in the sponsorship contract, but elements of the specific sponsorship agreements depend on the type of the sponsorship (e.g., elements of the personal sponsorship contract are usually not the same as the elements of the event sponsorship contract):[213]

---

208. N. Johnson, *Effective Sponsorship Contracting – A Legal Perspective* (12th ESCA Congress 2002).
209. A specific way of sponsoring a team is the so-called linkage contracts, under which a sponsored person changes its official name with which it competes.
210. Sport federations often use a so-called pool of sponsors. They categorize sponsors according to their financial input.
211. Sometimes public regulation restricts advertising some sorts of products on sporting events. For example, Slovenian Sports Act forbids advertising of products that are harmful to health (nicotine, alcohol).
212. So-called corporate naming rights, by which corporations pay so that names of stadiums and arenas are changed into their trademark names.
213. S. Gardiner, *Sport Law,* 448 (3rd ed., Cavendish Publishing Limited 2011).

- the rights being granted;
- product and/or service category;
- territorial issues;
- warranties (especially by the event organizer regarding broadcast coverage of the event);
- duration options and renewals of the sponsorship rights;
- financial terms and conditions;
- obligations of the sponsored party;
- obligations of the sponsor;
- public and product liability;
- insurance;
- indemnities;
- access to the venue and accreditations;
- event cancellation and 'force majeure';
- termination;
- post-termination arrangements and restrictions;
- options to renew; and
- applicable law and dispute resolution.

III. Merchandising

313. Clothes and other goods with names or logos of sport clubs, leagues and sport federations are usually commercially more valuable than the same clothes without them. Sport fans want to show others who they are cheering for, and in order to do so they are willing to pay extra. Selling such clothes and other goods or just allowing others to print and sell them is an important source of revenue.

314. A merchandising contract is a contract 'by means of which an owner of the mark grants entitlement to its use to another entrepreneur so that the latter may use it on his product which are of a considerably different form to the product for which it was previously registered'.[214] By the word 'mark' in this monograph we are referring to registered trademarks, registered names, copyrights and protected personality rights of individuals (so-called personality merchandising).

315. Just like sponsorship contract merchandising contract is a so-called innominate contract. Its content therefore depends on the will of the contractual parties and general rules of Slovenian Code of Obligations. To be capable of concluding endorsement contract, someone must of course have the right. We will shortly explain how these 'marks' are protected in Slovenian legal system.

214. M. Colucci, *Sports Law – Italy*, 119 (Kluwer Law International 2004).

A. *Personality Rights*

316. As it was already mentioned, personality rights are protected by Slovenian Constitution. They are immaterial, absolute and non-transferable rights[215] that belong to natural persons.[216] Personality rights do not need to be registered. Although these rights have an immaterial nature the main point of them in sports industry is their commercial exploitation. An individual has the right to control the commercial use of his or her name, image, likeness, voice or other unequivocal aspects of one's identity. With these we have already named some of the personality rights that are most commonly commercial exploited. Famous individuals will, of course, allow the commercial exploitation of their name, image, etc. only if they receive appropriate payment. In case of unjustified infringement against these rights they will be entitled to adequate damage compensation.

B. *Registered Names*

317. According to Slovenian Societies Act, a club or a federation that believes that the name of another club is no different from its registered name and this causes or is likely to cause confusion in the legal traffic, has the right of appeal against the decision of the registration authority that registered the latter club or federation. This appeal can be filed within six months from the registration. Infringement of the right to a registered name gives the affected association also the right to compensation for damages.

C. *Copyrights*

318. According to Copyright and Related Rights Act,[217] visual images or songs of sport clubs and federations (e.g., coat of arms, clubs anthem) can also be protected under the copyright rules if they can be considered copyright works. Copyright works are defined as individual intellectual creations in the domain of literature, science and art, which are expressed in any mode, unless otherwise provided by this Act. Copyright is consisted of three rights:

(1) an indivisible right to a work, from which emanate exclusive personal powers (moral rights);
(2) exclusive economic powers (economic rights); and
(3) other powers of the author (other rights of the author).

319. Copyright belongs to the author by the mere fact of creation of a work, so no registration is needed. A club or a federation cannot be the author since only natural persons that actually created the work are authors. This means that they have

215. These rights cannot be transferred as such, but their usage can be transferred.
216. A. Finžgar, *Osebnostne pravice*, 38–43 (Slovenska akademija znanosti in umetnosti 1985).
217. Official Journal of the Republic of Slovenia, Nos 16/07, 68/08 and 110/13.

to acquire the copyright from the author. Not all rights that constitute a copyright can be acquired, but economic rights that are most important for this monograph can. Economic rights protect the author with respect to his economic interests by giving the author an exclusive right to authorize or to prohibit the use of his work or copies of his work. If these rights are transferred, their legal holder can economically exploit them and in case of unauthorized infringement, he can claim for damage

D. (Trade)Marks

320. Under the Industrial Property Act[218] five industrial rights are protected: patents, supplementary protection certificates, industrial designs, marks and geographical indications. These rights are only protected by law if properly registered on either national or international level.

321. Eligible for registration as (trade)mark is any sign, or any combination of signs, capable of distinguishing the goods or services of one undertaking from those of another undertaking, and capable of being graphically represented, in particular words, including personal names, letters, numerals, figurative elements, three-dimensional images, including the shape of goods or of their packaging, combinations of colours as well as any combination of such signs. This means that names and visual images of sports organizations (associations and federations) can be registered as trademarks and in reality they are, for example, OCS, Slovenian Basketball Association, Football Club Maribor. Interestingly Slovenian Football Association and Slovenian Ski Association did not register their names and visual images as trademarks, but this does not mean that they are not protected by intellectual property rights, as they are protected by registered names and can be protected copyrights (if a visual image is an original work of the author and these associations have legally acquired copyrights).

322. One can wonder why an athlete, a club or a federation would register a (trade)mark and pay for the registration if more or less the same results can be achieved with other legal institutes that are acquired without registration and free of charge. The answer depends on the facts of each individual case, but the answer could be positive. (Trade)Marks are easier to prove, since they are registered, especially in case of counterfeiters that are very common in sports clothes manufacturing.[219]

---

218. Official Journal of the Republic of Slovenia, Nos 51/06 and 100/13.

219. In some cases sport clubs and also their sponsors could be pleased that their sports uniforms are being counterfeited since this increases the brand value. This especially applies to countries where residents cannot afford to buy originals.

IV. Ownership of Sport Clubs

323. Part I explains that sport clubs in Slovenia can only take the form of societies under the Societies Act, which logically means that they do not have partners or owners who could freely dispose of these clubs. This discourages wealthy individuals from investing in a particular sport. However, it was also pointed out that certain sports organizations allow clubs to set up a separate company through which they compete in membership competition, without it being necessary for sport clubs to be the sole members of such a company. This system, which is not state-regulated but based on autonomous sports rules, allows entry into ownership, but this is not exclusive.

Chapter 3. Private Regulation

§1. General Issues

324. Rules of sport federations and even individual contracts between clubs and athletes or sport federations and athletes often include legal norms with commercial law content. For example, sport clubs and sport federations restrict athletes in the selection of individual sponsors; athletes frequently allow clubs' and sport federations' economic exploitation of their personality rights. We shortly describe how these issues are regulated in Slovenian Football Association's and Slovenian Ski Association's autonomous rules.

§2. Football Association of Slovenia

I. Media and Television Rights

325. The Football Association has adopted special regulation on media and sponsorship rights in connection with football events.[220] If the Slovenian Football Association, as the organizer of the competition (national championship, cup), decides to jointly market media and sponsorship rights at matches, then individual clubs lose these rights. Such a decision is validly adopted only if the majority of clubs participating in a particular competition agrees to it. In the field of media rights, this allows the Football Association to sell the rights to broadcast all matches to one medium (e.g., television) and thus to obtain better business conditions and to broadcast more matches. The funds that the Football Association then raises in this way must be distributed among the clubs according to the formula. The decision then also sets out the obligations of the individual sport clubs hosting the match so that the medium can record and broadcast the match without interruption (e.g., providing recording areas, space for a commentator).

II. Sponsorship and Merchandising

326. Clubs and football players individually arrange their rights and obligations in contract that they conclude with each other.

327. Autonomous rules of Slovenian Football Association regulate legal relationship of this nature between football federation and members of national teams. As we have already mentioned members of national teams are obliged to participate in photo and video shootings for the needs of Slovenian Football Association's sponsors. It can be understood that members of national teams allow football federation to economically exploit their personality rights for the purposes of sponsoring national teams.

---

220. Available only in Slovenian language at: https://www.nzs.si/Doc/Arhiv/Predpisi%20NZS/17_-_PRAVILNIK_NZS_O_MEDIJSKIH_PRAVICAH.pdf (accessed 6 Aug 2020).

328. Regulation on media and sponsorship rights in connection with football events specifically regulates sponsorship rights and obligations related to the competition as such, and indirectly, also to an individual football match. Thus, the Football Association can agree that clubs must use the official competition ball, use the sponsor's logo on the equipment, place sponsor billboards next to the pitch, etc. Also, the funds raised in this way are distributed among the clubs participating in the competition according to a pre-arranged formula.

III. Ownership of Clubs

329. The rules on the licensing of football clubs allow a member team to compete through a related legal entity established in the form of a company. This is permissible if the club established in the form of an association is at least 26% the holder of the voting rights. This means that holders of 74% of the voting rights in that related party may be other entities. In this way, the autonomous rules of the Football Association indirectly allow ownership in a legal entity that competes.

§3. Ski Association of Slovenia

I. Sponsorship and Merchandising

330. Rules of Slovenian Ski Association only regulate legal relations between athletes who are members of national teams and sport federation regarding sponsorship and personality rights' issues. Relations between clubs and skiers are their own affair.

331. Rules on rights and obligations of alpine skiing national team's competitors[221] expressly state that by concluding a contract, the representatives transfer to the Ski Association all their material personal rights regarding the name and image, without any restrictions. This applies throughout the term of the contract. Regardless, the skier has the right to his own sponsor on the headgear, a personal sponsor and the right to additional promotion. All these are within the limits prescribed by the rules.

332. The shape, size and location of the promotional inscription on the headgear (helmet or hat) must comply with the rules. At the same time, the selected sponsor must not be in competition with the sponsors of the Ski Association. Before concluding a contract with a sponsor, the skier must inform the Ski Association, which must approve the contract. A skier can promote another sponsor (personal sponsor) on formal wear with the exception of jerseys. In this case, too, the inscription must comply with the rules and the contract with this sponsor must also be approved in advance by the Ski Association. In addition, a ski representative may also appear in

221. Rules of other skiing national teams are similar to alpine skiing rules.

the promotions of a sponsor, but in these cases he may not present himself as a representative or be dressed in the official clothes of the national team. During the term of the contract with the Slovenian Ski Association, skiers also have the right to develop their own brand, but they may not place it on the official clothes of the national team, except in the above-mentioned case. At the same time, a skier who wishes to enter into a car use contract with a sponsor must inform the Ski Association. It must present the terms of use and vehicle data in this notice. The Ski Association can offer the athlete an equivalent vehicle within fourteen days and the athlete must accept it.

333. Representatives are otherwise obliged to perform marketing campaigns for national team sponsors for a certain number of days without receiving a fee for this purpose.

II. Media and Television Rights and Ownership of Clubs

334. Ski Association of Slovenia does not have any rules on media and television rights or ownership of clubs.

Selected Bibliography

Avbelj, M. (ed.). *Komentar Ustave Republike Slovenije*, Part I (Nova univerza, Evropska pravna fakulteta, Nova Gorica 2019).

Bavcon L. et al. *Kazensko pravo – splošni del* (Uradni list Republike Slovenije, Ljubljana 2003).

Belopavlovič, N., Kresal, B., Kresal Šoltes, K. & Senčur Peček, D. (eds). *Zakon o delovnih razmerjih s komentarjem* (IUS Software, Ljubljana 2016).

Bergant Rakočević, V. (ed.). *Šport & pravo* (GV Založba, Ljubljana 2008).

Bergant Rakočević, V. (ed.). *Šport in pravo* (Inštitut za lokalno samoupravo in javna naročila, Maribor 2020).

Brajnik, R. et al. *Problematika delovnopravnega položaja športnih trenerjev s poudarkom na nogometu*, http://www.pf.uni-lj.si/media/zakljucni.izdelek.problematika.delovnopravnega.polozaja.sportnih.trenerjev.s.poudarkom.na.nogometu.pdf.

Chaker, A.-N. *Study on National Sports Legislation in Europe*. Council of Europe Publishing, Strasbourg, 1999.

Cigoj, S. *Komentar obligacijskih razmerij* (Časopisni zavod Uradni list SR Slovenije, Ljubljana 1984).

Crnić, I. et al. *(Uvod u) športsko pravo* (Inženjerski biro, Zagreb 2009).

Debelak, S. & Trstenjak, V. *Predpisi o društvih in ustanovah* (Uradni list Republike Slovenije, Ljubljana 1996).

Dolničar, J. *Statusnopravne oblike za opravljanje športa kot gospodarske dejavnosti* (Bachelor Thesis, Law Faculty in Ljubljana, Ljubljana 1996).

Đurđević, N. *Osnov odgovornosti za štetu koju pretrpi sportista na sportskom takmičenju*, 751–768 (Zbornik radova Pravnog fakulteta u Splitu, No. 4, Split 2012).

Gardiner, S. et al. *Sports Law* (Cavendish Publishing Limited, London 2005).

Grad, F., Kaučič, I. & Zagorc, S. *Ustavno pravo* (Pravna fakulteta, Ljubljana 2016).

Ivanjko, Š. *Predlog pravne organiziranosti nogometnih klubov v Republiki Sloveniji* (Unpublished paper written for Slovenian football association, Maribor 2007).

Jagodic, T. *Pravne značilnosti sponzorskih pogodb v olimpijskem gibanju* (PhD Thesis, Law Faculty in Ljubljana, Ljubljana 2007).

Jerman, S. *Razmejitev pridobitne in nepridobitne dejavnosti za potrebe obdavčenja nepridobitnih organizacij*, 183–199 (8. davčna konferenca Slovenskega inštituta za revizijo, Ljubljana 2008).

Jerman, S. *Spremembe in problematika obdavčitve nepridobitnih pravnih oseb po*

ZDDPO-2, 121–139 (10. davčna konferenca Slovenskega inštituta za revizijo, Ljubljana 2010).
Jerman, S. & Odar, M. *Zakon o davku od dohodkov pravnih oseb s komentarjem* (GV Založba, Ljubljana 2008).
Ješić, S. *Pravni vidiki uporabe nedovoljenih snovi v športu* (Bachelor Thesis, Law Faculty in Maribor, Maribor 2010).
Juhart, M. & Plavšak, N. (eds). *Obligacijski zakonik s komentarjem*, Book I (GV Založba, Ljubljana 2003).
Kirschenhofer, M. *Sport als Beruf* (Peter Lang, Frankfurt am Main 2002).
Kokalj, V. *Zakon o društvih s komentarjem* (GV Založba, Ljubljana 2006).
Konstandinović, S. & Konstandinović, I. *Pravo i sport* (Fakultet za menadžment u sportu, Beograd 2007).
Korošec, D., Filipčič, K. & Zdolšek, S. *Veliki znanstveni komentar posebnega dela kazenskega zakonika,* Book 2 (Uradni list Republike Slovenije and Pravna fakulteta Univerze v Ljubljani, Ljubljana 2019).
Milić, Z. *Sport i pravna regulativa u sportu* (Fakultet sporta i fizičkog vaspitivanja, Beograd 2007).
Novak, J. *Delovni spori* (GV Založba, Ljubljana 2004).
Novak, J. (ed.). *Zakon o delovnih in socialnih sodiščih s komentarjem* (GV Založba, Ljubljana 2005).
Nunič, M. *Zakon o javnih zbiranjih s komentarjem* (GV Založba, Ljubljana 2011).
Perović, S. & Stojanović, D. (eds). *Komentar Zakona o obligacionim odnosima*, Book I (Pravni fakultet Kragujevac, Kragujevac 1980).
Plavšak, N. (ed.). *Gospodarske pogodbe,* Book 2 (Gospodarski vestnik, Ljubljana 1994).
Plavšak, N., Juhart, M. & Vrenčur, R. *Obligacijsko pravo – splošni del* (GV Založba, Ljubljana 2009).
Podlipnik, J. *Status športnika v moštvenem športu primerjalnopravno in v slovenski zakonodaji*, 187–206 (Podjetje in delo, No. 1/2006, Ljubljana).
Podlipnik, J. *Obdavčitev dohodkov športnikov* (Master Thesis, Law Faculty in Maribor, Maribor 2006).
Podlipnik, J. *Pravni in davčni status športnih klubov* (PhD Thesis, Law Faculty in Ljubljana, Ljubljana 2010).
Podlipnik, J. *Davčna oprostitev za nepridobitne organizacije zasebnega prava v Sloveniji in izbranih državah*, 31–49 (Javna uprava 3-4, Ljubljana 2011).
Podlipnik, J. *Zakon o davku na dediščine in darila s komentarjem in sodno prakso* (GV Založba, Ljubljana 2013).
Radoševič, M. *Nekatera vprašanja pravne ureditve telesnokulturnih organizacij v SR Sloveniji s posebnim ozirom na košarkarske organizacije* (Bachelor Thesis, Law faculty in Ljubljana, Ljubljana 1984).
Sancin, V. *Mednarodno pravo v hierarhiji pravnih virov EU in njenih članic* (Uradni list Republike Slovenije, Ljubljana 2009).
Selinšek, L. *Kazensko pravo* (GV Založba, Ljubljana 2007).
Siekmann, R. *The Specificity of Sport: Sporting Exceptions in the EU Law*. Zbornik radova Pravnog fakulteta u Splitu 4, Split 2012, 697–725.
Šturm, L. *Zakon o društvih s komentarjem in vzorcem pravil* (ČGP Delo, Ljubljana 1975).

Terra, B. & Kajus, J. *Introduction to European VAT.* IBFD, Amsterdam 2011.
Travner, A. *Društva: nova zakonodaja* (Pozoj, Velenje 1997).
Trstenjak, V. *Pravne osebe* (GV Založba, Ljubljana 2003).
Ude, L. *Arbitražno pravo* (GV Založba, Ljubljana 2004).
Ude, L. et al. *Zakon o arbitraži s pojasnili* (GV Založba, Ljubljana 2010).
Vraničar, M. & Beč, N. *Zakon o davku na dodano vrednost s komentarjem* (GV Založba, Ljubljana 2007).
Zeilner, F. *Sport und Recht* (Peter Lang, Frankfurt am Main 2003).

Selected Bibliography

Index

The numbers here refer to paragraph numbers.

www.ingramcontent.com/pod-product-compliance
Lightning Source LLC
LaVergne TN
LVHW021112300926
849160LV00009B/709
* 9 7 8 9 4 0 3 5 3 1 5 0 2 *